Praise for Choose

"Starting a business can be incredibly hard—if you make the wrong choices. Make the right choices, though, and your idea can quickly become a highly-profitable, mission-driven business with raving fans. Ryan is a great business mentor and he'll save you a tremendous amount of time and money with this book."

— **Brendon Burchard**, #1 *New York Times* best-selling author of *High Performance Habits*

"For any entrepreneur who wants to start or grow a business, Choose *eliminates the fear and overwhelm by simplifying the process in a way you won't find anywhere else."*

— **Hal Elrod**, #1 best-selling author **of** *The Miracle Morning* book series

"Whether you're looking to start your first side-hustle or you are a serial entrepreneur looking to launch your next million-dollar venture, stop what you are doing and read this book right now!"

— **Kevin Harrington**, original shark from the hit, Emmy-winning show *Shark Tank* and author of *Key Person of Influence*

"Before you can scale up your business, you have to decide what business you're in. Choose *is a book every aspiring entrepreneur must read before launching their business or entering a new market."*

— **Verne Harnish**, founder, Entrepreneurs' Organization and best-selling author of *Scaling Up*

"Starting a business may be the riskiest thing you'll ever do. In Choose, *Ryan Levesque cuts the risk down to size, helping you make the single, biggest choice you face: selecting the right market. Get this book and get started!"*

— **Michael Hyatt**, *New York Times* best-selling author of *Your Best Year Ever*

"50% of Americans dream of starting their own business. But only 5% make that dream a reality because most are afraid or just don't know what to do or where to start. This book is about to change that second statistic forever."

— **John Assaraf**, *New York Times* best-selling author of *Having It All* and co-author of *The Answer*

"If I were starting out again, I'd be using Ryan's strategy to help me figure out and test ideas. His approach is straight out of *Ready, Fire, Aim*—adapted to today's amazing digital-based tools."

— **Michael Masterson**, best-selling author of *Ready, Fire, Aim*

"Ryan has reduced choosing your market to a sequence of precision quadrants that nullify your chances of diving into an empty swimming pool, breaking your neck, and plunging your family into ruin."

— **Perry Marshall**, co-author of *Ultimate Guide to Google AdWords* and *Ultimate Guide to Facebook Advertising*, and author of *80/20 Sales & Marketing*

"Choose passion. Choose creativity. Choose to grow. Choose your own business, your own success, and your own future. Choose to explore and experiment, to fail and then flourish. Choose meaningful over mindless. Choose to create a life that you love madly. Your first step? Choose this book, Choose."

— **Sally Hogshead**, *New York Times* best-selling author of *Fascinate* and *How the World Sees You* and CEO, *How to Fascinate*

"Ryan Levesque gives you something I've never seen before—a detailed process to analyze any business model and market, and systematically answer the single most important question . . . will this actually work?"

— **Jeff Walker**, author of the #1 *New York Times* best-seller *Launch*

"It will change the way you think about your past business failures, the mistakes we all make along the way, and what you could now do instead. This is the book you'll wish you had before you launched your first business and the one that will help you find that next level."

— **Dean Graziosi**, #1 *New York Times* best-selling author of *Millionaire Success Habits*

"*The mix of detailed, step-by-step instruction coupled with motivation, inspiration, and dozens of real-world examples instantly makes this the #1 book every aspiring entrepreneur's must-read before launching a new product or business.*"

— **Tom Ziglar**, CEO, Ziglar, Inc., proud son of Zig Ziglar, and author of *Choose to Win*

"*Chock full of actionable and applicable strategies, Choose will improve the odds of your successful business launch more than any other book I have read.*"

— **Mike Michalowicz, best-selling author of** *Clockwork and Profit First*

"Choose *gives you a blueprint for discovering a lucrative niche you can build a valuable business around.*"

— **John Warrillow**, founder, The Value Builder System™, and best-selling author of *Built to Sell* and *The Automatic Customer*

"*Anyone in business or starting a business will have such an amazing advantage with this book as their guide. Practical. Step-by-step. And laid out perfectly.*"

— **Garrett Gunderson**, *New York Times* best-selling author of *Killing Sacred Cows* and co-author of *5 Day Weekend*

"*Too many aspiring entrepreneurs focus on the wrong questions. Ryan Levesque's new book,* Choose, *is a game-changer for anyone who wants to start a business.*"

— **Dorie Clark**, author of *Entrepreneurial You* and *Stand Out*, adjunct professor, Duke University Fuqua School of Business

"*Millions of failed entrepreneurs would probably be successful ones today had they had Ryan's book as their guidepost and litmus tester. I strongly recommend the book because it makes logical/infallible predictable sense out of that which seems random.*"

— **Jay Abraham**, founder and CEO, The Abraham Group, Inc., marketing expert, and author of *Getting Everything You Can Out of All You've Got*

"This book flies in the face of the conventional wisdom about how to start a business. Required reading for anyone who is even thinking about starting a business."

— **Ray Edwards**, best-selling author of *How to Write Copy That Sells*

"Whether you're starting a brand-new business or expanding your existing business, Choose is an absolute must-read book for every digital marketer."

— **Ryan Deiss**, CEO, digital marketer, and best-selling author of *Digital Marketing for Dummies*

"If there was ever a book that should be read before any and all businesses are started, it's this one! Ryan does a fantastic job in helping you figure out not only what problem your business should solve, but also how to package, market and grow that solution, after the fact."

— **Chris Ducker**, best-selling author of *Virtual Freedom* and *Rise of the Youpreneur*

"Ryan Levesque nails it! Ryan's Choose Method is the simplest, lowest cost way to identify entrepreneurial opportunities and reduce start-up risk that I've ever seen."

— **Roger Dooley**, author of *Brainfluence* and *Friction*

"As an author and podcaster helping to serve aspiring entrepreneurs myself, Choose is a must-read for anyone not sure how to get started with their own business."

— **Pat Flynn**, *Wall Street Journal* best-selling author of *Will It Fly?*

"Ryan Levesque takes choosing the perfect market to an entirely new, practical level by giving you a formula, a system, and a way to rely on data (and not just your gut) to do the perfect research in order to make your biggest impact in the world."

— **Brian Kurtz**, Titans Marketing, serial direct marketer, and author of *Overdeliver* and *The Advertising*

"How do you figure out if your business idea is going to be a big winner or a waste of time and money before you even launch it? Ryan Levesque simplifies the process of starting a new business by showing you how to ask a simple set of questions in order to choose the right path."

— **Eben Pagan**, best-selling author of *Opportunity*

"Choosing what business or niche to go into, just might be the most important decision you will ever make as an entrepreneur. Choose is a rigorous methodology that is proven to work, and a must-have tool for anybody thinking of starting a new business whether it's your first or not."

— **Josh Turner**, *Wall Street Journal* best-selling author of *Connect* and *Booked*

"Ryan is one of the few experts who actually knows how to move the needle for business owners with his methods. This will save you years of heartache and fast-track you towards the results you deserve."

— **Nicholas Kusmich**, leading Facebook ads strategist and best-selling author of *Give*

"If you don't already have your offer that converts, this book will help you narrow down the possible opportunities to just the ones that matter."

— **James Schramko**, author of *Work Less, Make More* and founder, SuperFastBusiness

"The reason 90% or more businesses fail can be traced back to the very first choice the entrepreneur ever makes. I love this book because it helps save us, starting right from Day #1. Remember, if your first choice is not the right one, you don't stand a chance."

— **Anik Singal**, best-selling author of *eSCAPE* and CEO of Lurn.com

"Ryan's simple, four-step process makes it possible to 'choose' right the first time, eliminating the mystery in generating genius ideas, so start-ups gain immediate traction and achieve success quickly."

— **Annie Hyman Pratt**, former CEO, The Coffee Bean and Tea Leaf

"Ryan leads you through a paradigm-shifting breakthrough about choosing the right market, your overall business plan, and even understanding yourself better as an entrepreneur through this process."

— **Jason Friedman**, CEO of CXFormula, LLC

"I have started 12 businesses and sold 7 of them. Choose *is a must-read for anyone even thinking about starting a business today."*

— **Mark Timm**, exponential entrepreneur, president and CEO, Ziglar Family

"To deeply impact people's lives, you must get clear on who you're truly meant to serve. Not all markets are created equal. In Choose, *Ryan Levesque helps you discover the perfect audience for you."*

— **Selena Soo**, creator of Impacting Millions

"The insight and simplicity from the framework Ryan shares in Chapter 1 alone are worth the price for any newbie to veteran entrepreneur."

— **Todd Herman**, author of *The Alter Ego Effect* and creator, 90 Day Year performance system

"If you're the type of entrepreneur or elite executive who thrives on a methodical, systematic approach for assessing potential business opportunities, this book is like mecca."

— **Victoria Labalme**, performing artist and guide, strategist, and coach

Choose.

ALSO BY RYAN LEVESQUE

Ask

Choose.

The Single Most Important Decision
Before Starting Your Business

RYAN
LEVESQUE

HAY HOUSE, INC.
Carlsbad, California • New York City
London • Sydney • New Delhi

Published in the United States by: Hay House, Inc.: www.hayhouse.com®
Published in Australia by: Hay House Australia Pty. Ltd.: www.hayhouse
.com.au • **Published in the United Kingdom by:** Hay House UK, Ltd.: www
.hayhouse.co.uk • **Published in India by:** Hay House Publishers India:
www.hayhouse.co.in

Jacket and Interior design: Nick C. Welch

Library of Congress Cataloging-in-Publication Data

Names: Levesque, Ryan, author.
Title: Choose : the single most important decision before starting your
    business / Ryan Levesque.
Description: 1st edition. | Carlsbad, California : Hay House, [2019] |
    Includes bibliographical references.
Identifiers: LCCN 2019000163 | ISBN 9781401957476 (hardcover : alk. paper)
Subjects: LCSH: New business enterprises. | Business planning. | Strategic
    planning. | Entrepreneurship.
Classification: LCC HD62.5 .L4767 2019 | DDC 658.1/1--dc23 LC record
available at https://lccn.loc.gov/2019000163

Hardcover ISBN: 978-1-4019-5747-6
e-book ISBN: 978-1-4019-5748-3
Audiobook ISBN: 978-1-4019-5749-0

10 9 8 7 6 5 4 3 2
1st edition, April 2019

Printed in the United States of America

If you've ever had the crazy dream to start
your own business,

If you've ever dreamed of doing your own thing,

If you've ever failed, or lost it all on something . . .

In a quest to shake the status quo,

If you have something right now that *is*
changing the world . . .

But you don't know where to take it next.

Or if you're simply trying to figure out what
you want to do . . .

And who you want to *be* when you grow up . . .

This is the book *I* wish someone had written . . .

When I was where *you* are right now.

In short?

This book right here . . .

Is for *you*.

Contents

Start Here

Your Most Important Choice
Before Starting a New Business

What's the single most important question you should ask *before* you start your business?

Think about it for a second.

Any guesses what it might be?

Is it a question about yourself? A question about your experience?

Or is it a different sort of question altogether?

The actual answer might surprise you.

It wasn't immediately obvious to me when I first discovered it.

But when I did, that's the moment everything changed.

It's a lesson I'll never forget.

And it all started in the strangest way possible . . .

▲   ▲   ▲

The first business I started was selling instructional tutorials for how to make jewelry out of Scrabble® tiles. Sounds weird, right? It was a surprising turn of events, especially considering that only months before I had been making six figures at my finance job with AIG in China. I have the financial crisis of 2008 to thank for AIG nearly going bankrupt, and I have a trip to Malaysia while reading *The*

4-Hour Workweek by Timothy Ferriss to thank for my desire to find another way to work.

I had long been fascinated by China and jumped at the chance to work in the international finance and insurance world after graduating from Brown University. My wife, Tylene, and I quickly got married and moved overseas, with me in Shanghai and her in Hong Kong to get her Ph.D. Ultimately, the expat life wasn't all I thought it was going to be, and when I opened *The Wall Street Journal* one morning to see the headline that AIG was going under, I promptly handed in my resignation, sold everything, and moved to Hong Kong to reunite with my wife. We had some money but not a lot—certainly not enough for me to spend my days sightseeing. As a way to generate income, I launched the Scrabble tile business to piggyback on the growing fad my wife had discovered on Etsy. It eventually made me a few thousand dollars a month until the fad ended and business dried up.

Tylene and I moved back to the U.S. completely broke after burning through our savings. She landed a job as a curator at a museum in Brownsville, Texas, making $36,000 a year. Brownsville is a town one mile from the Mexico border and in the poorest zip code in the country. We lived in a rundown one-bedroom apartment with lawn chairs as our living room furniture. We were on a $50 per week food budget and bought all our groceries at Walmart, except for eating at the Stars Drive-in every Tuesday because they had $1 cheeseburgers. We bought three and split the third.

Despite our living conditions, my foray into the Scrabble business had armed me with enough hope that my entrepreneurial ventures had potential. I decided to launch my first real Internet business. I chose the obscure niche market of orchid care. Yes, it's a market and a very viable one at that.

After 18 months, I was making $25,000 per month.

I knew I'd stumbled onto something that was more than a successful venture. When I deconstructed the orchid care business—why it worked, why it would continue working, and whether I could replicate it in another market—I realized that my accomplishment could be traced back to one decision I had made that largely accounted for my success. More on that in a minute.

First, let's acknowledge this up front: Entrepreneurship is a risk. Out of the millions of people each year who take the leap of faith to start their own small business, about 20 percent fail in their first year and 50 percent fail in their fifth year.[1] If you're one of those who've already failed once, you know how hard that result can be on your confidence, and your wallet (and that's just for starters!). If you're not one of the 50 percent who've already failed, perhaps the potential of failure has you second-guessing the journey in and of itself. Maybe your life is pretty good right now and, if you're being honest, the thought of being in business for yourself is exciting, but the thought of losing the comfort and stability you currently enjoy is unsettling. Entrepreneurship always creates an internal battle.

There's no shortage of good business ideas or people with the drive to go after them. So why all the failure? How can it all go wrong when you seemingly do everything right? You may create a brand, produce your website, write your emails, make your product, utilize every resource you have, and spend valuable time and money (that you may or may not have), yet still not find success in your venture.

Some people blame the economy or business loan interest rates or bad decisions about vendors. Some people blame themselves, thinking, *If only I had worked harder or been more creative or were just more cut out for business.* I'm here to tell you that none of the above is what will cause your business to fail out of the gate. While there might be some contributing factors on that list, none of them will single-handedly determine your fate.

But there is one thing that will, and it's this: *choosing the wrong market.*

If you choose the wrong market, your business is destined to fail before you even begin.

Guaranteed.

The mistake of choosing the wrong market can be traced right back to asking the wrong question at the *very* beginning. I see it time and time again: the whole entrepreneurial process is doomed from the get-go because of one simple, avoidable mistake:

Instead of asking *what*—*what* should you sell or *what* should you build?—you should be asking *who*. As in, *who* should you serve?

The *what* is a logical question that will come soon enough, but starting off with *who* is the foundation from which all other things are built.

Whenever you enter a new market, it's like you're launching a boat on a river. If you've ever been rafting, you know that progress on the river comes in two ways: 1) natural current and 2) human effort. When launching, some people put their boats in a river with deep water and a strong current that propels them forward and pulls them into immediate forward momentum. Everything's accelerating so fast that it's sometimes hard to keep up, but it's the wild, wind-in-your-face ride every business owner seeks: problems of progress instead of problems of inertia.

On the other hand, some people launch their boats in a shallow river with only a ripple of current. While they might reason that they can make a big splash there, the reality is that after the initial splash flattens, all progress will require hard, exhausting work. Momentum will last only seconds before another burst of your energy is needed again.

If you choose to launch into a shallow, still river, the odds of success are not in your favor. Even if you buy the most expensive rafting equipment, hire the most capable crew, and bust your butt for 18 hours a day, if there's no natural current in that water, you're not going to travel far before lamenting that there has to be a better way.

At the same time, a river overflowing with raging white-water rapids can be just as problematic. *Too* much current can cause you to capsize or be swallowed up whole. And when a river becomes a really popular destination, it can quickly become overcrowded and uncomfortable. You definitely don't want to launch your boat in the middle of a traffic jam on the water.

But what if you knew where to find the hidden river that is "just right" for you to launch your boat? You'd still have to prepare your boat and get it to the river's edge, yet you'd be doing so with the confidence that once you launch, momentum will come right away. Success will be a matter of navigating the swift current, as opposed to spending all your time trying to generate one.

That's what this book is all about.

This book is for anyone who has ever dreamed of starting a business or doing their own thing. Whether that means potentially quitting your job and going *all in* or starting a side hustle on nights and weekends. It's also for anyone who's ever tried to start a business but either failed or struggled to get it to take off in a big way.

At the same time, this book is for anyone who is running a successful business right now and wants to either expand that business in a new market, or is possibly even considering starting a new, separate *unrelated* business. And finally, this book is for anyone who is still trying to figure out what they want to do and who they want to be when they grow up.

In short, this is the book I wish someone had written when I was where you are, right here, right now.

This book is going to help propel you forward in your journey. Not only will I be here to help make sure you put your boat in the *right* river with a current that's driving you where you want to go, but I'll be in the boat with you, as your river guide, through every page. I'll make sure you avoid the dangerous hazards of the rocky and treacherous waters, help guide every stroke of your paddle to ensure you're steering toward your desired destination, and set you up for success to build the business of your dreams.

I served over 100,000 entrepreneurs with my book *Ask*, in which I reveal the methodology I used to be successful in 23 different markets—from orchid care and memory improvement to weight loss and golf instruction. I loved hearing the thousands of success stories from readers who followed my process, like Charlie, who quickly grew his $10,000 per month guitar lesson business into a $2.5 million per year business, or Jamal, who went from making $17 per hour to earning $600,000 in his first 12 months. Despite hearing about all the wins, it would pain me to occasionally hear from a reader who had followed the ASK Method® to the letter and still struggled or failed because they unwittingly chose a bad market. I realized I had to write this book to explain something I *didn't* reveal in *Ask*: how I chose my successful markets in the first place. So in a way, this book is the prequel to *Ask*. The truth is that it's possible to do everything right from a tactical standpoint—use the right funding, hire the right people, launch at the right time—and still struggle to get your business off the ground and make money. And this will always be the case, without fail, if you choose the wrong market. This book is designed to help you avoid that fate altogether.

Even though I now find myself enjoying success in multiple markets and helping thousands of entrepreneurs confidently find and enter new market niches every year, when I was getting started, there were some very dark nights of agonizing over my first big market decision and second-guessing myself. One night I was lying in bed at 3:00 A.M., tossing and turning with worry. I'd found two markets I thought I could enter—bonsai trees and orchids—and was sweating over risking the time and money I was about to invest. Would it all be for nothing? Was I in over my head? What did I even know about bonsai trees or orchids? This was right after Tylene and I had moved back to the States. We were living off her modest $3,000/month (before taxes) museum income, and we hoped my small business success would allow us to start thinking about buying some indoor furniture for the living room, maybe even enjoying a nice dinner out once a month. The margin for error was small. If I failed at this venture, our lawn chairs in the living room were probably going to stay for a while. And I would be back to working a nine-to-five job. I wished there was some way I could have more certainty.

Nobody wants to put in all that time and effort and money and end up worse off than when they started—especially if life isn't all that bad right now. I've found that one of the biggest, if not *the* biggest, worries we face when launching a new business is losing the pretty good, stable life we already have. That worry can turn into insomnia really quickly. But it won't if you have confidence your business will find immediate momentum.

When it comes to choosing your market, validating your idea, and deciding what business to start, there are so many questions you might have.

How do you build a successful business that's not only about making money but has a purpose and is about helping people as well? Is there a way to leverage your existing market knowledge or expertise (and what if you don't have any)? How do you decide what type of business to go into if you're more introverted? What if you're more of an extrovert? How does your personality even factor into what type of business you can start? What if the buyers in your market aren't hungry for your idea? How can you differentiate and position yourself against your competition in a way that ensures your idea will be a winner no matter what? Is there a way to choose a market that has enough potential to keep generating revenue for the rest of your life? How do you overcome the feeling that there might be a better niche or business that you haven't thought of yet? Is there a way to decide whether you should niche down to multiple sub-niches or if you should focus on a more generalized message?

And what do you do if you're stuck or overwhelmed? Should you focus on following your passion and existing knowledge? Or on the size and potential of your market? And how do you choose your market if you do *not* have a strong passion driving you to any particular market or business? How do you choose your market when you're interested in a lot of things and it feels like there are too many options to choose from? What about when you're equally torn between two things you love? How do you get yourself to finally take that "leap of faith" if you're the type of person who thinks about things way too much and gets stuck in analysis paralysis? And how do you finally move forward and get started?

You might have a host of ideas, questions, and concerns bouncing around in your head, and the worst part of it all is that you're not sure where to start. You may be wondering: *What's a legitimate question and what's just fear based? What are the questions I should be asking, that maybe I'm not even thinking of right now? What's a solid idea and what's bound to be a flop no matter what I do? What matters most and what can wait until later?*

The good news is that this isn't my first trip down the river. I've guided thousands of entrepreneurs through the process we're about to embark on together, and I've successfully done it solo two dozen times myself. Along the way, I've made all the expensive, painful mistakes so you don't have to. And those questions above? I've *also* had to address every single one (and many more) at some point along the way.

Between my own journey and coaching thousands of entrepreneurs through *their* journey, I couldn't stop thinking about the need for a framework: some type of system that could guide you through the appropriate questions and give you confidence that you have found the right answers. Maybe something in stages so you wouldn't move on to the next phase until you completed the phase before it. Something based on actual hard numbers, rules, metrics, trends, and conditions with clear checkpoints that would make it obvious whether an opportunity was a clear go or a no-go. Something foolproof.

This obsessive compulsion to succeed comes from an honest place; I was a kid from a working-class family who always had something to prove. I was the smallest player on my soccer team, the band member who played two instruments but neither very well, the spelling bee contestant who made it to state competition and then failed miserably. I'm not saying it's the healthiest mindset, but I felt like I never quite measured up, so I obsessed about how to grow as quickly as possible in every area that mattered, and some that didn't. I'd hacked my way to becoming my soccer team's captain, leveraging speed over size. I discovered in 9th grade, much to my surprise, that I was ranked #1 academically in my high school class—certainly not because I was naturally "smart," but because I studied like crazy and frankly was deathly afraid to fail. Eventually, this same drive became the compelling force that pushed me to figure out how to succeed as an entrepreneur. But, of course, I didn't just want to succeed once; that wouldn't prove much. I wanted to figure out how to do it again and again. I became consumed with uncovering the strategy to do just that. And just for good measure, I did it 23 times. That is what mastery is all about.

After *Ask* was released and I saw that people were still making the one fundamental mistake of choosing the wrong market, I knew it was time to create a shareable process that could solve the issue once and for all. This was the beginning of a three-year journey where I poked and prodded and tested and refined a step-by-step process that would give you the best rate of success when it came to choosing your market and starting your business.

I started by dissecting my own decade of experience during which I had entered dozens of different, unrelated markets and generated over $150 million in revenue, building multiple businesses and even landing on the *Inc.* 500 list of the Fastest Growing Companies in America. But I zeroed in on my failures as much as I did on my successes, maybe even more so, especially in the early years. Where had I gone wrong? Could I have done anything to prevent them? Were there common denominators among all the ventures that thrived, and all the ones that crashed and burned? I compiled my findings, tested my initial hypotheses by entering several markets as my own guinea pig, and then started using the methodology with a handful of my own clients: I was fascinated to see that what I shared was often the last missing piece that helped them unlock success.

I then began sharing the methodology with entrepreneurs around the world and started teaching it online. Each time I coached people through the process, I circled back to tweak and hone the content to make sure it was streamlined, relevant, digestible, and applicable; answered the pressing questions; and addressed the biggest pitfalls. Again, and again, and again. All of this is to say that the Choose Your Market journey you're about to dive into is based not just on my own personal experience, but on the results of literally thousands of students and entrepreneurs around the world who have now used this methodology to launch and grow successful businesses (some of whom you're going to hear about in this book).

It's through that same Choose Method™ that you're going to learn how to measure demand for your idea, determine market size and potential, and find your unique angle. We're going to cover the best way to evaluate your competition, determine how narrow your focus should be, choose the right business model, and decide what to sell and how much to charge. You'll discover how to incorporate your passion and purpose, what to do when you feel stuck or overwhelmed, and how to finally move forward and get started with a business idea that's worth pursuing in a market niche that has legitimate success potential, even if you're the type of person who tends to ponder way too much and get stuck in analysis paralysis.

The process we're about to embark on together is a three-stage process: the Brainstorm stage, Test stage, and Choose stage. Each of your business ideas will be run through these successive stages; individual results will be the determinant in moving forward with confidence to the next step or going back and rethinking your idea or approach.

Here's a quick overview of the process:

STAGE 1—BRAINSTORM

- ☐ Step 1—Model Brainstorm
- ☐ Step 2—Market Brainstorm
- ☐ Step 3—Business Idea Brainstorm

STAGE 2—TEST

- ☐ Step 4—Bullseye Keyword
- ☐ Step 5—Market Size Sweet Spot
- ☐ Step 6—Market Competition Sweet Spot
- ☐ Step 7—Market Must-Haves

STAGE 3—CHOOSE

- ☐ Step 8—Choose Your Market
- ☐ Step 9—The Final Step to Launch

Obvious definitions aside, the Brainstorm stage allows you to start wide and gather all your potential ideas, ensuring that you don't narrow your thinking at the outset. The Test stage is where you'll vet your brainstormed ideas by pitting them against proven industry standards to assess their potential. The Choose stage is where you'll take your Test results and make an informed decision that enables you to either choose your market and move forward with clarity and confidence, confidently set the idea aside, or confidently alter the idea and place it back into testing. Effectively, each stage lays the groundwork for the next stage until you can make your ultimate choice with certainty.

To further guide you, I'll be providing various resources—including worksheets, graphs, lists, assessments, and bonus materials—that will help drive these points home and further the exercises and explanations.

I'll introduce each of these resources in the chapters where they are most useful, but an easy way for you to find the various resources throughout the book is to look for this icon:

Anywhere you see this icon indicates you have access to additional, exclusive resources to support you through the process over in your Bonus Online Resource Area at www.choosethebook.com/bonuses.

Downloadable and printable versions of each worksheet mentioned in the book can be found there. You can also find full-color versions of all the graphs and screenshots in this bonus area (in particular the Google Trends graphs really come to life when you can see each of the keywords as its own color). Additionally, you have access to a handy compilation of all the resources summarized in one location at the back of this book for your reference.

One of the key things you're going to have to land on up front is your business model: the way in which you're going to go about generating revenue and profits. When you're an entrepreneur, it can feel incredibly overwhelming to be faced with the sheer number of options out there. In the name of transparency, know that I'll be steering you toward my recommended choice of selling *education and expertise*. That is, finding people who want to buy your ideas, information, and/or expertise (or the expertise of others). Another key point I want to dive into is a concept that's integral to the Choose Your Market process, specifically during the Test stage. It's based on something you're already very familiar with: the traffic light. Yes, as in: Red for stop, Yellow for caution, Green for go. Using this rudimentary notion takes all the guesswork out of evaluating which of your brainstormed ideas are viable. You'll weed out ideas that turn out to be Red lights, treat ideas with caution if they turn out to be Yellow lights, and move forward confidently with ideas that turn out to be Green lights. If you hit a Red light at any point through the test process, you'll go back to your brainstorm ideas and run another idea through.

Now, to the importance of mindset. Since some parts of this process are going to feel counterintuitive and uncomfortable, there are a couple of things that will be helpful to bear in mind.

Embrace iteration. You might need to loop back around a few times if the first markets you brainstorm don't pass the Red light, Green light test. While that might make you feel like you're going backward, you're actually making progress. Sometimes you have to go back before you can go forward.

What you say no to is perhaps even more important than what you say yes to. It's addition by subtraction. You want to eliminate possibilities because that will get your business going faster. You actually want some of your ideas (or almost all your ideas) to fail. So reframe failure as progress, which understandably may be hard since some of your ideas might be things you've thought about your whole life, and it's a crushing blow to find out they're not viable. I've definitely been there multiple times—but trust me, it's better to know now rather than after your business fails to grow.

Finally, to make any type of progress, you must acknowledge that you have to start somewhere. What do Elon Musk, Steve Jobs, and Sara Blakely all have in common? They all used to *not* be billionaires. Those highly influential and successful entrepreneurs all started from scratch, with nothing, because that's where most entrepreneurs start.

The biggest mistake you can make when studying successful people is to look at what they're doing now instead of what they were doing when they were at the stage you're in right at this moment. Despite the odds and many setbacks, they chose to push through the unknown. They chose to keep going in the name of passion and progress. They chose resilience over fear. And of course, they chose the most important thing of all—the right market.

I've been down this river before. Many times, in fact. And I've guided many entrepreneurs through this same exciting, terrifying, and thrilling journey. Here in this moment is where that journey begins for you. So strap on your life jacket and grab your paddle, because we're about to go for one heck of a ride together.

Are you ready?

Let's jump right in . . .

STAGE 1

BRAINSTORM

You don't have to get it perfect.
You just have to get it going.

Even if the best ideas drop out of the sky and into your lap, they most likely require some tweaking. When's the last time your first draft was final, or your first take was a wrap? On the road to choosing your market, there are a handful of foundational decisions you need to make. And even if you think you already know what those decisions will be, there is way too much value lost if you don't give yourself the opportunity to brainstorm.

Have you ever heard of the British rock band Pectoralz? Me neither. What about Starfish? Those were the two original band names of Coldplay. Same for the mega-successful band Nirvana. Before they cracked the "big time," the lead singer, Kurt Cobain, made a demo tape under the name Fecal Matter, and then multiple names followed, including Skid Row and Ted Ed Fred. Even the iconic band KISS didn't start out with that name. They used to make the rounds on the New York music circuit as Wicked Lester. The band Goo Goo Dolls was forced to find a new moniker after a club owner refused to put The

Sex Maggots on his marquee. Van Halen originally called themselves Rat Salad.

And that, my friends, is the importance of brainstorming. If everyone went full steam ahead with their very first ideas, we might all be going to see the Rat Salad reunion tour on Friday night.

The act of brainstorming is not a new or revolutionary concept. The term made its debut in the 1940s in a book by advertising executive Alex Osborn, who was developing methods for creative problem solving.[1] Since then, it's become an increasingly buzzworthy technique. There are group brainstorms (Google swears by them); solo sessions (Yoshiro Nakamatsu, the inventor of floppy disks and owner of over 3,000 patents, goes deep sea diving to come up with new ideas); exhaustive open-ended exercises (Upworthy requires their writers to come up with a minimum of 25 headlines for each article); and timed discussions (Microsoft alum Nicole Steinbok says to keep brainstorm sessions to 22 minutes). The tactics may differ but the purpose remains the same: Gather ideas. Iterate. See what resonates; see what doesn't.

Some people get overwhelmed at the mere mention of brainstorming and claim they're not creative enough for idea generation. If you put yourself in that category, you're not giving yourself enough credit. Have you ever named a child or a pet? Have you thought through multiple routes to get to a location? Have you come up with a theme for a party? Have you written an email and then rewritten the first line? In all of these scenarios, your brain is managing ideas and then filtering them. That's brainstorming.

All you have to do is apply that same line of thinking to the next three steps where you'll decide on your business model, niche market, and business idea. They will be the infrastructure upon which choosing your market and starting your business will sit, and through explanations, examples, and pointed questions, I'm going to help you vet and polish them.

Ready?

I officially welcome you to the think tank.

Model Brainstorm

If you want to build a house, you wouldn't lay your foundation and start erecting walls without first having a blueprint. Just as building a house requires a blueprint, building a business requires one too. Your business blueprint is otherwise known as your business model, and it's the first decision you have to make when moving forward with your entrepreneurial endeavor. It's the plan that shows how everything is supposed to work, and it provides the structure and parameters you'll need in order to confidently break ground.

I won't downplay the importance of weighing all your options when it comes to choosing a business model. I'm all in favor of making informed decisions, and I appreciate anyone who does their due diligence in investigating the best framework for their business. Do you set up a physical storefront? Do you start selling physical products online? Do you become a real estate agent? Do you do affiliate marketing? Do you set up a restaurant? Do you run a done-for-you marketing agency? It feels like the number of options is endless. At the end of the day, each and every type of business model allows you to create and deliver value to your customers, and all include varying degrees of compensation and trade-off.

For example, if you set up a physical storefront, you've got rent and a fixed location. You get to have face-to-face interaction, but can only sell to people who are in your geographic area, and that's incredibly limiting. There are also significant expenses associated with managing inventory, working with suppliers, and hiring employees—all of which are still payable whether or not sales are strong.

Maybe you decide to sell e-commerce products online; that sounds really good. Only to realize that if you sell $100,000 worth of product, you then have to factor in all your costs—manufacturing, cost of goods sold, distribution—which means you might end up walking away with only a few thousand dollars in your pocket.

You might think you want to set up an agency, doing something like marketing or public relations. That's all fine and good, but doing work for other people is often a roller coaster ride. Some months you might have more work than you can handle and you can't even get to all of it, and other months you're wondering where your next client is going to come from. It becomes doubly problematic when you have employees, and you have to staff up when you need more bandwidth and then lay people off when there's not enough work. It can be a very painful place to be.

Perhaps you set your sights on software. The profit margins can be enticing when you think about income streams like advertising income and monthly recurring revenue. But you might have turned a blind eye to the huge up front (and often continual) costs associated with software development, licensing, distribution, advertising, and customer support staff, not to mention the servers, data security, and other tech. I once joked with a client that if you want to start a software company, the path is simple: take a million dollars in cash, light it on fire, and once the smoke clears, then you can get started.

When you look at all these possibilities, you have to wonder—is there an option that's the perfect place to start? Is there an option that is truly the *best* business model? And I will make an argument that there is one business model that rises above all the others, and it's this: selling *education and expertise.*

I believe this is the most practical and foolproof option for anyone looking to find immediate success as an entrepreneur. It's the crux of the methodology that I teach through my ASK Method training. It's much faster than building physical products, which require production, importing, and shipping (as opposed to expertise, which can be a digital product). Second, it's the most cost-effective business model of the bunch. There are few to no development costs since you can build products yourself without much investment—e-books, a YouTube channel, or digital downloads, to name a few. Because *education and expertise* can be marketed exclusively as an online product, you also eliminate additional costs associated with maintaining retail space and stock, i.e., no dreaded inventory management and dealing with SKUs. The net? The ability to launch quickly with low operating costs contributes to a high profit margin right away.

In contrast with physical e-commerce, where you might only pocket a few thousand dollars on $100,000 in sales, when you're selling *education and expertise,* almost 100 percent of that $100,000 can land in your pocket. In concert with that benefit, consider that in 2011, around $35.6 billion was spent on self-paced e-learning worldwide.[1] By 2015, that number had more than quadrupled to $165.2 billion and it's expected to reach

$275 billion by 2022.[2] In short, people are spending on *education and expertise* at historic levels.

Obviously, you should launch the business model best suited to you, and the Choose Your Market process will still be applicable. But if you're open to it, I would strongly recommend you consider selling *education and expertise.*

The most common hurdle people have to overcome when it comes to the *education and expertise* business model is the word *expertise.* In my experience, few people consider themselves experts. We tend to devalue our own unique combination of experience and accumulated knowledge. We think, *Well that's obvious! Everyone knows that.* But here's the thing: they don't.

The fact is that everyone has a strength they can capitalize on, and to the many who believe they have to be the foremost in their field in order to be considered an "expert," I say you need to change your mindset. There are millions of people out there who seek knowledge or guidance for the sheer purpose of understanding fundamentals. They don't always require mastery of a subject.

Consider that you'd be hard-pressed to find someone who hasn't gone online and typed "How to . . ." into Google or YouTube. From hobbies to home projects, practical health advice to mechanical instruction, we live in the Information Age, when people seek answers for themselves. Yes, there is a lot of free information that's out there. And it's shrewd to wonder how you can still make money in markets where there is a lot of free information. But there is still an abundance of money to be made by those who can differentiate themselves, inject their personality into their content, and deliver the real answers or solutions people are seeking. People like Lex Case, who educates gardeners on how to grow better organic tomatoes online. And Alexis Fedor, who teaches thousands of artists around the world how to turn their art into a business. And Kristi Kennedy, who produces digital programs for children, parents, and elementary schools to help kids recognize, prevent, and recover from bullying. And Ron Reich, who provides dog owners with online resources to help them potty train their puppies.

Ron was an attorney who practiced law for a couple of years in California until he knew that being a lawyer didn't fulfill him like he thought it would. So he went looking for something else, something that would give him freedom and allow him to make an impact. He ended up entering the "potty train puppy" market and created an online business that serves dog owners and their furry friends.

The point I want you to see here is that you don't need to have a Ph.D. in a subject to have something to offer. Or you can have a Ph.D. in something entirely different and decide to go a different route. I have plenty of clients who pursued earlier careers because they thought that's what they were "supposed to do" (nurses, attorneys, family business—the list goes on), only to arrive and then wonder what else was out there.

When Charlie Wallace started his online business, he was just a guy who knew how to play guitar. You might know a dozen people who know how to play guitar, and maybe some of them even play pretty well. But if you got an itch to learn yourself, wouldn't you consider asking one of them for some advice? After all, they know more than you do. They can play, for starters. You can't. Charlie used this simple premise to launch a business that delivers guitar lessons online. He followed the steps you'll learn in this book, and people liked what he had to offer. He now has had over 200,000 aspiring guitarists worldwide use his guitar training.

If Charlie had gone the brick-and-mortar route, he'd have faced much higher overhead costs with an office lease, and his lessons would only be offered to his local community. Instead, using technology, Charlie has been able to adapt to a purely online expertise model, achieving a much larger reach and much higher revenue than he would if he were selling guitar lessons out of a local shop. Today, he could buy his own building if he wanted. Instead, he just bought his dream house.

If you're still struggling with the idea that you have expertise to offer, consider that you can always learn how to do something that others would like to know. When I sold how-to information on making Scrabble tile jewelry, I wasn't the guy who invented the machines that mold and form each tile in every Scrabble game in the world. But I knew, from my wife and based on spending a little time on Etsy, that a *lot* of people were making jewelry out of Scrabble tiles. And I knew if I could learn how to do it myself and then simplify that knowledge into a practical digital tutorial that was slightly better than the competition, I potentially had something to offer.

Back in my college days, I chose neuroscience as my major at Brown, and in that first week of my freshman year, all I could think about was how I was completely in over my head. Not only did all the other kids seem so much smarter than me, but the classes associated with my major were, in a word, intense. Even the Intro to Neuroscience class was hardcore, not counting the added pressure that it was a prerequisite for moving forward with my major.

I lived in fear that entire first semester. I'd go to the library and sit in the "Absolute Quiet" room, which was soundproof and buried underground. That's where I studied incessantly and that's where I earned my A grade. In fact, I didn't score below a 98 percent on any exam in that class.

Fast-forward two years and the faculty put out a call for a student to teach a section of that same Intro to Neuroscience class. To be considered, you had to have been in the top 3 percent of the class when you took it. Because I had studied my butt off, I fell into that percentile. But teaching it was a whole different story. I was hardly qualified. What if I was in the middle of teaching and someone asked, "What does this mean?" I was crazy to entertain the idea, yet I felt drawn to the opportunity.

So I did it. I threw my hat into the ring and was chosen to lead and teach a section of class that year. The self-imposed preparation that followed was epic. Even though there was a lesson plan for the semester, I wanted to genuinely understand what I was teaching. I dedicated countless hours to reviewing and memorizing important concepts covered in the textbook, and actually felt pretty good about it by the time the first class rolled around. Little did I know that my obscene amount of textbook preparation wasn't all that necessary.

If you don't think you're ready to teach someone, think again. The simple act of teaching will raise your expertise exponentially, in a way you didn't even think was possible. Just the need to simplify information into bite-size morsels for others to easily digest is a valuable undertaking. I didn't have a Ph.D. or a master's degree, but students would come up to me and say they learned more from my class than they did from the head of the neuroscience department (who wrote the textbook) because he was so deep in the weeds. After asking the students why, I learned that it wasn't really my vast knowledge of the textbook that was so helpful; it was that I was able to deconstruct the information into a form they could grasp. I had struggled and really had to work to learn the material that I could relate to them. Meaning: if you've ever had to struggle to learn or do something, that can actually put you at an *advantage*. An expert can be nothing more than a learner teaching other learners. *To a 4th-grader, the 5th-grader is a genius.* You just need to stay one step ahead, not necessarily light-years ahead.

The idea of capitalizing on your expertise doesn't need to cause sleepless nights. And if you're still unsure of yourself, you can always consider partnering with someone you know who does have a certain expertise to share. What can they teach you? Would they like to join forces? Maybe they're the right brain to your left, or vice versa. Brainstorming your business model also means brainstorming how to make the model work for you.

In fact, if you already have an existing business with a different business model, selling *education and expertise* can also augment your existing products or services. A brick-and-mortar stationery shop could also run workshops on productivity hacks or organizational planning. An e-commerce site that sells fitness products could offer online training for running a marathon. A software company offering a health and wellness app could also offer live counseling sessions over your smartphone. A done-for-you social media agency could also sell DIY social media online courses and workshops.

The options are endless, and we'll begin brainstorming more ideas in the next chapter. For our purposes, let's assume you're going to launch an *education and expertise* business model, or at least expand your current other model by also selling *education and expertise*. The next question is: How are you going to sell your product? (Note: even though the word *product* may conjure up something tangible, in this instance it represents anything that incorporates your expertise.)

When it comes to selling *education and expertise*, there are four product categories you can explore. Based on the specific goals of your business, and even your personality type, one or more of these will rise to the top. I've broken them all down into what I call the Product Grid™.

ⓑ Product Grid

When it comes to selling *education and expertise,* there are four product categories you can explore. A downloadable version of this Product Grid is featured in the Model Brainstorm Worksheet available in your Bonus Online Resource Area.

Product Focused

The *Product Focused* option quite literally means you're focused on productizing your expertise. The "product" can be physical, like a book, but in this day and age it is most often digital, like an e-book or online course. This is all about achieving scale and is an ideal option if you want to reach and impact the largest possible number of people. The trade-off with this option is that you're not working with any one particular individual face-to-face, in a deep, extended way. You provide something that's accessible to a large number of customers, potentially anywhere around the world. Just like this book, for example.

This option offers you *consistency* through the opportunity to generate evergreen revenue. If you offer something like a digital course that you can sell every single day, it gives you a consistent income and consistent sales that you can rely on to serve as the foundation of your business.

Through my work in the orchid care market, we offer a physical book, a digital book, and online digital courses. It's self-sustaining, and after the initial content generation, it can be pretty hands-off if you want it to be. Or this quadrant can be a doorway into the other quadrants in the Product Grid.

Client Focused

The *Client Focused* quadrant, as the name suggests, is about the client. This option includes things like private consulting, hosting a mastermind group, or running a group coaching program. And in contrast with the *Product Focused* quadrant, it typically has you serving a small number of clients at a time but working with them in a deep and intimate way.

One of the biggest benefits is that you can impact your client's life or their business (if you serve them in a business context) in a direct and often deep way. It's typically the best way to pilot new programs, try out new ideas, and generate new *case studies* that you can then use for testimonials and success stories in your marketing.

My ASK Method business works in both the *Product Focused* and *Client Focused* categories. We offer a physical book, digital courses, and online masterclasses, but there's also a business coaching program, as well as a high-level mastermind group. While the two quadrants are very different from one another and can successfully stand alone, they can easily be combined to work in tandem.

Membership Focused

The *Membership Focused* option is about building a community of people, typically online. Things like membership sites and online networking groups that are designed to generate *continuity* income. A prime example is a chamber of commerce. Between local, city, state, and national chapters around the world, there are over six million[3] small business owners who pay a monthly or annual membership fee to a chamber of commerce so they can be part of a community of other like-minded individuals—that is, small business owners just like them.

I talked about the *consistency* that your Product Focused quadrant can deliver by generating new sales day in and day out, but the *Membership Focused* quadrant can generate one sale that pays you over and over again. If you have an online membership site that requires a monthly membership, people sign up once and then continually pay you. It also serves to build your community of people because now you have an audience, and to that group of people, you can introduce new products or new Client Focused opportunities.

Event Focused

The fourth and final quadrant is the *Event Focused* option. Examples include workshops (which can be virtual), boot camps, or in-person live events—basically, any concentrated event where people are getting together in one place and that begins and ends within a succinct period of time.

This last option is designed to give you *concentration*. There's no better way to get your entire community—the group of customers you serve—all focused on one thing than to host an event. It can be a physical meetup or a virtual, online summit; the point is that it's a gathering of like-minded people with you at the helm. And whatever expertise you're selling—how to grow a business, improve health, care for orchids, build Scrabble tile jewelry—that will be the focus of the event. There's no better way to build a concentration of energy.

When you look at each of the four quadrants on the Product Grid, it's interesting that each one represents a different level of *introversion* or *extroversion* in terms of your personality. Let's take a look at that for a minute. An *extrovert* generally refers to someone who tends to be an outgoing, overtly expressive person who derives energy from being around and interacting with other people. Alternatively, an *introvert* tends to be more shy and reticent, especially around large groups of people, and recharges and derives energy from being alone. Largely speaking, very few of us are extreme introverts or extreme extroverts. Many of us fall at some place on the spectrum in between. Although we can each demonstrate introverted and extroverted tendencies at various times, we do generally tend to prefer one over the other. The satisfaction, happiness, and joy that you derive from your business can in many ways come from making sure the business you start is in line with your personality.

Let's face it: If you're an introvert and you like to be by yourself, and you're building a business that requires you to be in front of thousands of people every single day, are you going to derive satisfaction and fulfillment from that business? It's unlikely that you will. Similarly, if you're more extroverted and you build a business working from home, spending your days alone behind a computer screen, you're probably going to be craving more human interaction.

If you're *very* introverted (which I refer to as "double II"—a double introvert), you may consider building a Product Focused business. It's an ideal route if you prefer to create something and then manage it from behind a computer screen and not have to present to or be in front of an audience on a daily basis.

If you're slightly *less* introverted (a "single I"), you might look to the Membership Focused quadrant. You can largely work from behind closed doors, and inter-act with people digitally through a message board, in a forum, or in a Facebook group. You don't necessarily have to meet people in person or get on the phone, although you certainly could. In our business, our ASK Academy membership and community fill this quadrant.

If you're on the extrovert side of the scale ("single E"—a first-tiered extrovert), a client-based business could better suit you. This option calls for someone who enjoys spending considerable time interacting with clients. You're working with people, typically in the form of phone calls, Skype meetings, or Zoom communication, so it requires that you tap into an extroverted side of yourself.

And finally, as you can imagine, hosting an event means you have to be your *most* extroverted self (you guessed it—"double EE"). Revolving your business around the Event Focused quadrant means you're typically either speaking in front of your audience or managing the event, working the room, answering questions, and making people feel comfortable and heard. At The ASK Method Company, our annual events and conferences bring together thousands of readers and like-minded entrepreneurs (and *aspiring* entrepreneurs) from around the world to connect and meet in person. For me and my role, this means I get the opportunity to do everything from teaching on stage to sitting down and meeting some of my readers in person. It's a role I enjoy tremendously, but from sunup to sundown, it certainly requires being on your extroverted A game!

So the question is this: Which quadrant do you feel best fits your personality?

Of the four categories we just covered, can you see how each quadrant might interact with the others as you start building out your business? It's like a giant meal that can be served à la carte. It can be customized to meet the needs of what you're selling. You can choose to line it up with your product, your personality, your lifestyle, or your availability. Or all of the above. If you're torn between two or more, you can always choose a primary quadrant in which to start your business, and then expand into other quadrants over time. This is exactly what I did. So the question is this: Which quadrant speaks most to you? Which one is feasible when you take into account your capacity and skill set?

Your answer does not need to be set in stone at this exact moment. You're just thinking about the possibilities, so you can begin to envision what your business might look and feel like. This whole section is designed to make sure all your foundational pieces fit together to form a solid base, and that can often require some maneuvering. It helps to begin with the end in mind and know some of the decisions that you will need to make down the line. As we move through the next two steps, feel free to circle back here and reevaluate. This flexibility is a huge part of the value of this whole brainstorming process.

🔖 The Model Brainstorm Worksheet includes a version of the Product Grid we just covered, outlining the various models that might apply to your situation or expertise. Feel free to refer to it for review, to utilize it to help sketch out what your business might look like, or to simply jot down some notes. For your convenience, it is listed in the back of this book along with all the other bonus resources, and it is available now for you to download and print at www.choosethebook.com/bonuses.

IN/UP/MAX

I'm a big believer in beginning with the end in mind, so before we move to the next brainstorming step, I'd like to share a helpful concept I use with my coaching clients after they've chosen their market. It's a progressive framework we call IN/UP/MAX, and here's how it works.

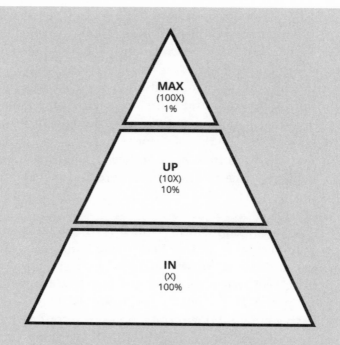

A more detailed version of the IN/UP/MAX Framework is outlined in the One Page Business Model Worksheet available for download in your Bonus Online Resource Area.

When you launch your business, you generally aim to usher customers into your business ecosystem by selling a low-priced product that offers a low barrier of entry for 100 percent of your customers. This is called your IN.

Once customers have been introduced to your business or brand, you can then begin offering a more premium product at a higher price, roughly 10 times the cost of the entry-level product. This is your UP, and whereas 100 percent of your customers will purchase your IN product, generally speaking, only 10 percent of your customers will purchase your UP product.

Finally, there is one more tier of customers who will pay top dollar for your product or service. While they only represent approximately 1 percent of your total customer base, it is to this customer segment that you can sell your MAX product at a value of roughly 100 times your IN product.

The prices at each of these levels are different from one market to another. Let me give you a tangible example so you can begin thinking about how this can play out in your business. In the orchid market, your IN might be a downloadable $20 e-book that informs customers how to care for their orchids. Your UP might be a $200 digital course that shows customers not only how to care for their orchids, but also how to initially choose a good orchid at a local florist, and then how to properly repot or plant your orchid in a garden. And finally, your MAX might be a $2,000 greenhouse kit.

In a business-to-business consulting practice, your IN might be a $100 digital course, your UP might be a $1,000 half-day consulting session, and your MAX might be a $10,000 retainer or annual contract.

All this is to say that as you move closer and closer to choosing the right market for your business over the coming pages, you can simultaneously begin mulling over what your IN, UP, and MAX might be. While your business should generally (but not always) start with your IN, I've found that it's helpful to keep the path ahead in mind so that when you finally choose your market, you'll already have an idea of what your UP and MAX might be as well.

Now it's time to take Step 2 of the Brainstorm Process—brainstorming your market. Here, I'll share a few examples of profitable niche ideas from a vetted list I kept secret for years, paired with a practical guideline for determining which market best suits your interests and match what we call your Entrepreneur Type. Knowing your entrepreneurial tendencies ensures your business choice will play to your natural strengths, harnessing your efforts and energy in the right direction and setting you up to build a fulfilling business that you enjoy. When you align your entrepreneurial strengths with the right market and right business idea, you will not only have the best chance to succeed, but the best chance of building a business you love.

Market Brainstorm

At this point you're going to take the idea of the expertise model and whatever specific quadrant(s) from the Product Grid you're leaning toward and put them in your back pocket, which is where they'll live while you brainstorm some initial thoughts about markets. And by the way, if you're not sure which type of product is the best fit for you and your business based on your personality, your goals, and your objectives, I have a free assessment you can take to help you discover the business and product that's right for you, inside the Bonus Online Resource Area.

Okay! Ready for some fun? This is when you get to bring your passion, skills, and expertise to the forefront and use them to start spitballing markets you may want to focus on. What market will you choose? It's the million-dollar question, with a million ways to go about answering it. But the first place we're going to start is with *you*. When you think about it, starting with you is a really logical way to go about all of this. Not only will you be the one running your business, but unless you want an uphill battle where every decision goes against your grain, taking your strengths and talents into consideration isn't selfish; it's sensible.

So here we go: What type of *market* best suits the type of *entrepreneur* you are?

Out of all the entrepreneurs that I've had the honor of coaching over the years (as well as observations from my own experience), I've found there to be four main types of entrepreneurs.

⏱ The 4 Types of Entrepreneurs

Mission Based	Passion Based
• Called to pursue a specific mission	• Something you love
• What you would "Die on the Hill" for	• A deep interest
• Strong moral compass	• You want to share with the world
• Move away from something negative	• Move toward something positive
• Make a positive impact	• What you're excited about
Opportunity Based	**Undecided**
• Motivated by growth	• Know you want a business
• Find and follow new ideas	• Not sure what that business will be
• See potential in unsatisfied demand	• Open to ideas and direction
• Drawn to unsolved problems	• Uncertain about path
• Solve a practical problem	• "Practice Business" an option

Understanding which of the 4 types of entrepreneurs you are will help guide your choice of business model, product, and market. A downloadable version of this table is available in your Bonus Online Resource Area.

Mission Based

The *Mission Based* entrepreneur has a clear and specific mission they feel called to pursue; their cause is one they would "die on a hill" for, and their business, therefore, is centered around it. Mission Based entrepreneurs see some *wrong* in the world that they want to make *right*. It's safe to assume most of these entrepreneurs have a strong moral compass or, at the very least, a desire to make a positive impact, which often revolves around solving social problems or effecting social change. Sometimes (though not always) they believe the mission comes before the money; as in, get the mission right and the money will follow.

A member of my ASK Method Business Coaching Program, Kristi Kennedy was a single mother of five. While her children are now grown, each of them experienced bullying and abuse in their youth, especially her son, who had suffered from severe autism. One day, after hearing about an especially disheartening incident involving her son, she'd had enough. Kristi refused to stand back and do nothing while children (hers or others') felt unsafe at school or were made to feel unworthy by their peers.

She created a bully prevention program that began as a traveling school assembly called the Bee Friendly Boot Camp™ (www.beefriendlynow.com) that teaches about value and belonging and fosters a culture of belonging, kindness, and character. Ten years later, Kristi still sits at the helm of Bee Friendly, which now offers year-round digital curriculum, products like Bee Affirmed Cards that instill words of encouragement, and a peer-to-peer Bee Buddies program for special needs students. A mission that started in response to a sense of duty has grown to serve thousands of kids at hundreds of schools.

Do you feel a strong sense of mission and purpose about something? Do you feel called to champion a particular cause?

Passion Based

In contrast, the *Passion Based* entrepreneur is fueled by a passion that revolves around a topic or subject matter they love, including anything from fishing to photography. In contrast to the Mission Based entrepreneur, who has a mission to right a wrong in this world, the Passion Based entrepreneur wants to share their passion with the world and transform it into a business. Mission Based is all about serving by moving people *away* from something negative, whereas Passion Based is all about serving by moving people *toward* something positive. When I first met Charlie Wallace, he was a couple thousand dollars behind on his rent and sleeping on a broken fold-out couch. Even though he was an extremely talented guitar player traveling the world with his band, the gigs didn't pay a whole lot, and he was struggling to make ends meet. He felt like the inevitability of putting down his guitar and getting a "real" job was fast approaching, but he couldn't stop wishing he could come up with a way to capitalize on his passion for playing music.

Knowing that the world was moving online and utilizing the Internet was going to be the most cost-effective way for him to reach people, he told his band he was going to start offering online guitar lessons. He dedicated time and resources to building a website, and www.guitarmasterymethod.com was born. Feedback immediately poured in that his teaching was producing real results for his customers. The first thing he did with the proceeds of his business was buy himself a bed.

Passion is contagious and can be a key ingredient in driving customer loyalty. Charlie's enthusiasm about playing guitar set him apart and made customers feel connected to his brand. They believed that he truly "got" them. Within just 12 months of launching his business, he was able to afford his dream home, complete with an in-house music studio. Starting with nothing, he's become a millionaire before the age of 30. And today, he makes seven figures a year while tens of thousands of guitarists use Guitar Mastery Method for its online catalog of guitar courses, one-on-one support team, members-only community via a private Facebook group, and VIP Club that offers monthly live lessons with Charlie.

What are you deeply passionate about? What is a subject or something that you are excited by or an outcome you would like to see in your life or share with the world? If you build a business this way, with the goal of tapping into and sharing that deep interest with the world, you're a Passion Based entrepreneur.

Opportunity Based

The *Opportunity Based* entrepreneur is one who finds and follows a new area of opportunity and growth. They see potential where there might be an unsatisfied demand in the market, and are typically the ones who think to themselves, *How has someone not solved that problem yet?* Unlike Mission Based entrepreneurs who are drawn to fight for a cause for which they would die on the hill, or Passion Based entrepreneurs who are drawn to transform or incorporate a life passion into their business, Opportunity Based entrepreneurs are drawn to solving a practical problem they've come across that represents an unmet need in the marketplace.

Dana Obleman was a brand-new mom with a baby who wouldn't sleep through the night. As anyone with kids can attest, sleep deprivation can lead to unspeakable levels of frustration, devastation, and—let's be honest—hallucination for everyone in the house, whether that be Mom, Dad, siblings, or pets. Plus, parents often feel like failures because they always thought babies were supposed to sleep a lot . . . hence the expression "sleep like a baby."

After Dana managed to solve her son's nocturnal issues and had him sleeping eight hours at a stretch without waking up, she and her husband Mike created The Sleep Sense™ Program (www.sleepsense.net) to make sure every parent who struggles with sleepless nights could get the help they needed. Through a downloadable e-book, they share a simple step-by-step process tailored to specific age ranges, as well as access to a 14-day video training course with in-depth "how-to" lessons with Dana. More recently, they implemented tiered membership that offers tons of additional bonus content.

The Sleep Sense Program has now been going strong for over a decade, served more than 79,000 parents, and been featured on national media like *Good Morning America*, CNN, *The Washington Post*, *HuffPost*, and WebMD. All because Dana was a blurry-eyed new mom who saw an opportunity to help parents who were in a similar predicament.

What opportunities do you see around you? Is there something you've identified that you could provide a solution for? If so, you're an Opportunity Based entrepreneur.

The final type is the *Undecided* entrepreneur, and they're the ones who aren't sure about most things related to deciding what type of business to start. They might not know what type of entrepreneur they are, they might not be sure whether they have a viable mission or passion worth pursuing, or they don't know if they are sitting on an opportunity worth building a business around. I'm raising my hand because this describes *exactly* who I was after I quit my job in Shanghai and moved to Hong Kong to be with Tylene.

With the end of Tylene's doctoral program imminent (followed by a probable move back to the States) and not wanting another corporate career, I had decided to work for myself. I was knee deep in researching various entrepreneurial market opportunities when Tylene offhandedly mentioned jewelry she'd seen selling on Etsy. They were Scrabble tiles with origami paper glued onto them using resin, and based on the vast supply of origami paper designs, the personalization was endless.

Living in China meant we had access to two things: 1) copious amounts of origami paper and 2) highly affordable labor. Tylene and I could practically see each other's wheels turning. We could buy supplies, hire people to make Scrabble tile jewelry, and sell the jewelry online with enough of a markup to turn a profit. But when it came down to it, I didn't want to tie us to a factory in China; I wanted to build a location-independent business. One that would let us travel. One that would let us live anywhere in the world. The idea was officially dead in the water.

Three weeks later, Tylene brought it up again.

"I thought we shut the door on that?" I asked.

"No, I came across something else," Tylene said. "There's this woman and she's not selling the jewelry, she's *teaching* people how to make the jewelry."

I looked into it, and sure enough, the woman was selling a how-to manual for making personalized Scrabble tile necklaces. I bought the product and was floored by how bad it was. Typos and blurry photographs—the whole thing was a lesson in poor quality. Which wouldn't have been a big deal had she not been charging $30 per download. She was robbing these people blind! Me included! But people were still buying.

On Etsy you can see how many sales the vendors are making, so we saw that this woman was generating between 10 to 15 sales each day. I did the math real quick. She was making around $300 a day—or $10,000 a month—selling a crappy PDF.

"All right, Tylene," I said with a mix of resolve and defeat. "Let's give it a shot."

I made the jewelry several times so I could properly articulate how to tell somebody else to make it; in other words, I was just trying to become the 5th-grader to my 4th-grader customers. My wife then took photos of each phase in the process and compiled it all into a professional-looking and user-friendly downloadable resource. I was pretty proud of the end product, actually. It was certainly better than the other one I'd seen. We started selling it, and within weeks it was generating for us a few thousand dollars of income per month. At its peak, we were clearing nearly $10,000 per month. And then, fads being what they are, the Scrabble tile jewelry craze ended and our revenue steam dried up just as fast as it had begun.

Undecided

Undecided entrepreneurs aren't rare. In fact, they may be the most common type of first-time entrepreneur. New endeavors breed uncertainty, and anyone who decides to brave a whole new world doesn't always know the ins and outs of what they're getting into, nor do they know just what it will bring out in them. How can people give themselves the best shot at success with so many unknowns?

Of the different types of entrepreneurs we just reviewed, which one jumped out at you the most? Did any of the descriptions feel like they were written about you? If you're like most people, you might have felt like you could relate to more than one type of entrepreneur, but we all tend to have one dominant type. And so, if you had to choose just one, which one would you say best describes you? Did any of the motivations (mission, passion, or opportunity) align with something you'd want to pursue? Or, like me when I started, are you unsure about where you fall? Which is absolutely fine. If you're curious to discover what type of entrepreneur you are and what type of business is right for you, I have a free assessment you can take inside the Bonus Online Resource Area.

If you're feeling undecided right now, and none of the other three types are really connecting with you, the important thing is not to let it stop you from progressing forward with this process. In time, you'll start gaining more clarity. Perhaps a couple more questions will do the trick. (It may be helpful to list out your answers. Lists have proven very beneficial for me.)

What are you naturally good at? What do people regularly ask you for help with? Maybe it's handyman-related stuff, or cake decorating, or copyediting, or makeup advice. What do you find easy that others might find hard? Have you succeeded at anything in that vein in the past?

What do you have expertise in? I know, I know, you may think you don't have any. So, let's reframe the question: What qualifications do you have? What jobs have you held? What have you researched and learned about?

What is the one thing you could teach someone if I told you that you only had ten minutes to prepare?

Who do you love to serve? Are there particular groups of people you're drawn to, maybe who are a particular age, or who are dealing with a specific challenge or situation? Maybe you resonate with people who have a particular personality, or financial profile, or are from a specific geographical area. What service do they need?

🪙 As you're thinking through all this, it might be helpful to access the Market Brainstorm Worksheet over in the Bonus Online Resource Area. This gives you a place to make notes as you go through this chapter. This worksheet is a starting place for you to begin thinking about the market you might want to focus on. Remember, it is a "brainstorm," so there are no "bad" ideas. Just get all your thoughts down as they come to you, and don't worry too much at this stage about "vetting" what you add (there's another step in the process I will guide you through to help you do that). For now, what you want to do is capture as many ideas as you can as you go through this process.

You never know when a good idea will hit. Mine tend to come in the middle of the night, or while I'm going for a run, driving my kids to school, or even taking a hot shower.

Do you remember the night I was tossing and turning at 3:00 A.M. trying to choose between the bonsai tree market and the orchid market? I knew next to nothing about either of them, but I'd done extensive research in the months following my short-lived success with the Scrabble tile jewelry business (which was both the driving force and the cause of my anxiety when it came to taking the plunge with another business). My research resulted in a list of dozens of possible niche markets I could explore, and bonsai trees and orchid care were both on there.

Let me back up for a second so you can appreciate how mundane brainstorming can seem . . . and how serendipitous it can turn out to be when you trust the process.

Back when I was living in Shanghai, I was sitting in my apartment on the 23rd floor and staring out the window at the smog. I was trying to brainstorm possible business ideas and was looking all around me for some thought starters. My eyes moved from the smog, to my living room wall, to the picture frame hanging on my living room wall, to a pillow sitting on an armchair in the corner, to a potted orchid sitting on the kitchen table.

Despite our best efforts, Tylene and I always managed to kill orchids. They were our favorite flower—despite or maybe because of their fragility—and every time one died, we just bought another. Seeing it there on the table prompted me to wonder if there was a secret to keeping them alive, and then I found myself adding "orchid care" to my list of markets.

That's it. I wish I could pretty it up for you, but I literally looked around my apartment and saw an orchid.

It wasn't a eureka moment. More importantly, I didn't stop my brainstorm right then because it was such a fantastic idea or I had a gut feeling that I had just landed on the key to my future. I didn't even look at that list again until we moved back to the States. And even then, orchid care was buried at number 57 in the pages and pages of possible market ideas. But by that time, I had a couple more tactics under my belt and a better idea of the requirements a niche needed to meet in order to be successful. And according to all of those criteria, the two markets that rose to the top of that entire list were bonsai trees and orchids.

It was as if someone was asking me if I wanted to eat glibbertygib or boobittybop for dinner. How was I supposed to know the answer if I didn't know what either was? The pressure to find "the one" felt almost paralyzing. There was a lot at stake—money and pride, just to name two—and I felt like I had only one chance to get it right. Then it hit me, the ol' middle-of-the-night idea: What if I treated this as my *practice* business? What if I chose one and went full steam ahead, but intentionally used it as a way to figure out the kinks? If things went well and I made money, that would be awesome. If things went south and I didn't find any success, I would have learned so much along the way. And whatever money I invested in the business I would just treat as "tuition." After all, I could either spend $250,000 to go and get my M.B.A., or invest a fraction of that to launch this business and quite possibly learn as much (or maybe even more) in the process.

That line of thinking took the pressure off having to get it right, and that wiggle room is what allowed me to spring into action. By the time the sun rose the next morning, I had chosen orchid care as my practice business, and my goal was to learn, improve, and get better results than I had with the Scrabble tile jewelry. As it turns out, my orchid care "practice business" went on to generate $25,000 a month in income within my first 18 months, and eventually generate half a million dollars a year, providing a level of financial freedom I had never dreamed possible as a blue-collar, working-class kid. In many ways, it was worth quadruple that amount in experience alone. I went on to enter many markets using what I learned in that first go-round.

No one hands a student driver the keys to a Ferrari. Teenagers need to go through years of trial and error before they're ready to handle the road in their dream car. They should start with a car that can take a few scratches to practice with, one that they (or the holder of the title) aren't completely attached to. Oftentimes in business, beginning by being dispassionate about the topic or subject allows you to become passionate about the *process*. Today, my passion is serving entrepreneurs around the world through my role as CEO of The ASK Method Company, but that wasn't my first business or market.

I hope you hit it out of the park on the very first pitch. I hope you choose the perfect niche market that aligns with your strengths as an entrepreneur and allows you to produce a product you believe in that reaps all the financial benefits your heart desires. I'm going to give you access to every tool in my arsenal to help make that happen. But in case it doesn't, know that it's a normal outcome and, as my own story illustrates, an important outcome. Remove the stress of thinking you need to have everything figured out, and watch how much easier things fall into place.

(Ⓢ) The Market Brainstorm Worksheet reiterates what we've just covered. In it, you'll find succinct one-liners to describe the four types of entrepreneurs—which may help you further determine which one you are—followed by pointed questions to help you continue to home in on your strengths and see how they can be applicable to your Entrepreneur Type. If you don't already have it, the full worksheet with its detailed instructions can be downloaded and printed from the Bonus Online Resource Area at www.choosethebook.com/bonuses.

STEP 3

Business Idea Brainstorm

The entire point of this first stage, and the most important thing to remember as you enter Step 3, is: *Brainstorm.* Embrace the level of freedom the brainstorming process affords you. This is all about capturing possibilities, so don't worry too much about filtering or critiquing your ideas. Know that there are no bad ideas, only good ones. Throw as many as you can against the wall and see what sticks.

Now that you've brainstormed potential market ideas, it's time to home in on your business idea. That is, what kind of business within your market might you create? Not sure yet? I'll be introducing you to some concepts to help you get clearer.

We started broad by brainstorming your overall model, and then moved into brainstorming your market. Based on the exercises, questions, and examples that were covered in Step 2, you hopefully came up with some market ideas that center around what you're passionate about and/or areas you have skill and expertise in.

Maybe you realized that your friends are always asking you to help them set up their Internet, or give them business advice, or share one of your famous cookie recipes. Maybe you found that you're passionate about helping first-time mothers, or teenagers heading to college, or farmers who want to switch to organic farming methods. These are all potential clues to help you determine your business idea.

Now we're going to take the information you've gathered and the strategic thinking you've already done, and go one level deeper. Welcome to the concept of *Keyword Phrases*. Yes, you already know what keywords and phrases are, but in the context of the Choose Your Market framework, Keyword Phrases have a very specific meaning that is fundamental to the whole process. Keyword Phrases are going to be the output of this current Business Idea Brainstorm step, and will be used to create a succinct and simple summary of your business idea.

Your Keyword Phrase might be how someone describes what you do, or what is at the core of what you offer. For example, your business idea could be to help people care for their orchids, teach the basics of playing guitar to amateur guitarists, run a doggy day care, or assist people in improving their memory. Keep in mind that the more specificity you can apply to your ideas, the better.

Keyword Phrases are a critical part of the Test stage, which we're rapidly approaching, and will ultimately help you determine which idea will provide the deep, fast-moving river you're looking to launch your boat into. Plus, your Keyword Phrases will also help you discover which ideas might be currentless rivers with no real forward movement, and which ideas are massive oceans with too much space to gain any real momentum. Suffice it to say, it'd be a good plan to take some time to think through as many Keyword Phrases as possible around your business ideas, with the goal being to whittle them down and move forward with your top three to five contenders. So let's brainstorm possible ideas. For example, if you're looking at the "public speaking" market, you might come up with a list of Keyword Phrases ranging from "how to speak in public" to variations on that theme, such as "presentation skills" and "speechmaking" or even more specifically, "presentation skills for beginners."

If you're struggling to come up with Keyword Phrases, an easy way to stir up more ideas is to type your first Keyword Phrase into Google, then scroll down and look at the "Searches related to" section at the bottom of the page, where you will see a list of other related Keyword Phrases.

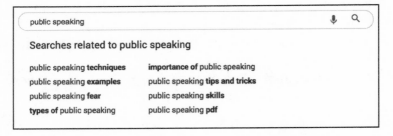

An easy way to get more ideas is to type your first Keyword Phrase into Google (for example, "public speaking"), and then scroll down and look at the "Searches related to" section at the bottom of the page.

Based on the results for a Google search on "public speaking," you could also add "speaking techniques" and "speaking skills" to your list of possible Keyword Phrases. You can also do the same using an online thesaurus, as the example below shows, to get ideas on a variety of possible related Keyword Phrases.

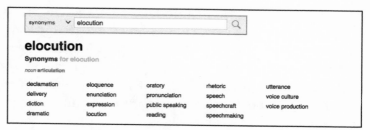

Another easy way to get more ideas is to type your first Keyword Phrase (for example, "public speaking") into a thesaurus to get suggestions on related terms.

In this case, the thesaurus results for "public speaking" could give you the idea to add "diction," "voice production," and "speechcraft" to your list of Keyword Phrases.

Once you have a comprehensive list of Keyword Phrases, you will need to do one more step. It may seem like a small thing, but it will make a big difference in everything that comes next. And that is to look at each Keyword Phrase on your list and transform it into an "I want to" statement.

You do that by completing the statement "I want to help people . . ."

Some examples based on various missions, passions, or opportunities would be:

"I want to help people *decorate their home.*"

"I want to help people *create better Facebook Ads.*"

"I want to help people *improve their relationships with their teenage children.*"

"I want to help people *get a job.*"

"I want to help people *paint their first watercolor painting.*"

Everything that follows after "I want to help people" becomes your Keyword Phrase that you will take into the Test step.

In my orchid business, my "I want to" statement was "I want to help people *care for orchids.*" So my Keyword Phrase was *"care for orchids."* For my RocketMemory™ product, it was, "I want to help people *improve memory.*" My Keyword Phrase that I took into the Test step? You guessed it. *"Improve memory."*

You'll notice we're not just saying "help people with *orchids*" but help people *care* for their orchids. Not just "help people with *memory*" but help people *improve* their memory. Keep this in mind as you're brainstorming your possible "I want to" statements, which will also come into play in the next step in the process. For now, the key takeaway is this: you want to be general but specific.

Now it's your turn.

Ⓢ To help you, I've put together the Business Idea Brainstorm Worksheet, which gives you space to list several potential business ideas. It begins with the prompt "I want to help people . . ." You can list your Keyword Phrases (as the completion of that "I want to" statement) on the left-hand side. Then, if you look to the right-hand side of the worksheet, you'll see the various criteria we covered in the Market Brainstorm step—from Mission to Passion to Opportunity Based entrepreneurs—and additional elements that pertain to your talent, expertise, and people, each of which will help you assess how specific business ideas align with those preferences.

If you wrote down, "I want to help people *brew their own beer*," you might feel that Passion, Talent, Expertise, and maybe even People could all be applicable to that business idea.

"I want to help people *recover from a stroke*" may check the Mission, Passion, and People boxes.

"I want to help people *raise bees in their backyard*" may check the Talent and Expertise boxes.

Ⓐ Overwhelmed? Don't worry about trying to evaluate or second-guess your ideas at this point; simply capture them on the worksheet. Then put a checkmark on the preferences that apply to that idea, and tally up the checks at the end to see which ones check the most boxes (literally and figuratively). Of course, the goal is to ultimately choose a business idea that has the highest score—once you check the boxes on the worksheet that apply to each idea, you can see which ones garnered the most checks and therefore are the front-runners. You can access a printable, downloadable copy of the Business Idea Brainstorm Worksheet in the Bonus Online Resource Area found at www.choosethebook .com/bonuses.

Checked boxes aside, there are two additional questions you can ask yourself if you're still unsure whether you want to even entertain a particular business idea. First: Does it suit your personality? Will this idea make you put forward a brand or message that's congruent or incongruent with your personal approach and style? Is one of your ideas a controversial topic that's going to require you to put yourself out there in a way that your beliefs will be challenged and you'll constantly be challenging others' viewpoints? Are you looking at ideas that require you to share aspects of your personal life that you might not be comfortable sharing with the public?

These are the types of things you want to be thinking about in terms of whether your business ideas resonate with your personality.

Second: Can you see yourself doing this in five years? Projecting forward and seeing yourself doing something not just today or next month, but for the next five years can be a great litmus test as to how interested and invested in an idea you might be. If the thought of doing something for the next 1,800 days immediately makes you feel miserable, it's safe to say maybe that idea isn't your answer.

Let's pause here. You're going to need to take your top three business idea Keyword Phrases into the Test part of the process. Have three come into focus based on the exercise above? If you're torn between more than that, feel free to take up to five with you. If you have fewer than three, or maybe even none, I'm ready to step in and help. This whole thing can feel confusing or overwhelming, and when that happens, sometimes it's nice to be handed a cheat sheet.

After having success in a few different markets, I started to discover the common criteria you want to look for before entering any new market. I went through one of the deepest, most rigorous research projects I've ever gone through in my entire life and came up with a list of the most lucrative, profitable niche markets that I would go into if I had the time. Markets that had proven to withstand the test of time. For years, I kept this top-secret list tightly guarded. It represented my business plan for the next 25 years; I intended to go into niche after niche after niche. Since then, plans have changed. I've shifted to teaching and serving other entrepreneurs around the world to help them choose the right market and start the right business. And yet, each time I revisit my hard-earned list, even all these years later, it holds up. The methodology behind it has ensured its relevance, and that's all the more reason to put it to good use.

Ⓢ So here's the thing: For the first time ever, I've decided to reveal 25 of the most lucrative, profitable niche ideas on that list. I've included those lucrative niches in a resource in the Bonus Online Resource Area that you can access at www.choosethebook.com/bonuses. In the meantime, to whet your appetite and give you a clue as to what some of those niches are, here are five of the niches on my top-secret list. Check them out:

1. Newborn photography
2. Transcendental Meditation
3. Speed reading
4. Grow vegetables
5. Listening skills

Let me guess—you can't believe that some of what you just read are considered niche markets. I'm right there with you. Or I *was* right there with you until I learned that all of these markets are not only real, but viable. If you can dream it, people just might want it. And if people want it, you're in business.

Up until this point, the examples you've heard for specific "I want to" statements are pretty straightforward in the way they translate to a niche market. Wanting to help people brew their own beer is a clear shot to the home brewing market, and wanting to help people decorate their home is obviously the home decoration market. But it's not always so cut and dried, and that's precisely why the "I want to" statement exercise lives in the brainstorm stage. It's a great tool to help you think through business ideas, but it doesn't always end there.

When I met ASK Method Masterclass student Robert Torres, he worked as a marketing director for a real estate company. His primary role was taking photos of various listings and making sure they were seen by potential buyers and sellers. Within the first nine months of being employed there, he generated 600 leads for the agents in the office. When those agents went on to only convert one percent of the leads, he stepped in and figured out a solution that immediately began to increase their conversion rates. That was the good news. The bad news was that Robert's manager informed him that converting leads wasn't his job; photography and generating leads was.

Robert was torn. These agents had become his friends, and he wanted to see them succeed, which would be all the more probable with each conversion they made. That's around the time he started studying my work. And right after I met him, his statement to me was "I want to help real estate agents convert leads." It's a great start. Once you know *who* (real estate agents), the question becomes *how*? How do you create a product from an idea? And *what*? What product do you even create?

A few years back, one of my "I want to" statements was "I want to help businesses create a warm personal touch in a cold digital world." That could have translated to a whole slew of things, but ultimately it's what led to the creation of my bucket.io® software company. Sound like a weird endgame? After all, my statement wasn't anywhere near "I want to help people survey and segment their customers using software."

My business idea was broad yet detailed, which meant I got to explore and organically see how it manifested. And here's how it played out: I realized that it all started with entrepreneurs better understanding their customers so they could better sell and better serve them. This is where using surveys came in. But not just any surveys; it's the nuances that matter. This is where the ASK Method—the subject of my *first* book—was born. I discovered the biggest challenge entrepreneurs faced was having the right technology and tools to not only survey their customers to better understand them, but to segment them into different "buckets" so they could customize their messaging in such a way that allowed them to create that warm, personal touch.

And it worked.

The book *Ask* became a number-one national bestseller, selling well over 100,000 copies, and my bucket.io software company now serves thousands of customers around the world, from first-time entrepreneurs who are just getting started and figuring out what market to go into and business to start, to large multinational corporations trying to better understand their customer base so they can ultimately better sell and better serve.

But back to Robert. After his "I want to help real estate agents convert leads" statement, he decided to start out with a practice business, Real Traffic Online, a media company centered around real estate photography. As a young husband and new dad, as well as having barely bounced back after other entrepreneurial attempts, he was hesitant to take too big a risk. What if he didn't make money? What if he didn't really have an expertise, but just got lucky that one time helping agents convert their leads? What if he wasn't equipped to run the show? You name it; he worried about it.

Well, his practice business ended up being the perfect move because it inadvertently became phase one of a much bigger master plan. You see, a quality real estate photographer can get agents more listings and can also increase the rate at which those listings sell (additionally, Robert offered drone videos to his list of services, which really took off . . . pun intended). As his client base grew, so did their leads. And you know what Robert could then swoop in to offer them? A way to convert those leads.

A year into running his successful practice business, he officially launched his Passion Based venture. The People and Properties Academy is an online community where real estate agents can come and learn for themselves how to generate and convert leads. Through tiered monthly membership that provides varying levels of supplemental support, they can get as much or as little help as they'd like.

Robert and I had similar business ideas as far as "better serving" goes, but they resulted in markets and outputs that couldn't have been more different. It just goes to show that you can have similar dreams, concepts, or objectives as someone else, but your specific skills and solutions are what will set you apart. If you think your "I want to" statement is one that a ton of other people will have, know that the difference can be found in your edge. (Although a ton of other people having the same idea could actually indicate an oversaturated market, in which case, I'll help you re-brainstorm.)

For now, let's circle back to your business idea Keyword Phrases. Do you feel good about the ones you have? Again, ideally you have three that you can bring with you into the Test stage. Heading there means we're at the end of the first phase of the Choose Your Market framework. Let's take a look back over the key insights we've covered in the Brainstorm stage so you feel good about moving forward.

By now, you're familiar with the need to have a business model that provides a strong foundation in order for you to find immediate success as an entrepreneur.

You've learned about the types of products or services you could deliver in your business by moving forward with the selling *education and expertise* model in one or a combination of four quadrants on the Product Grid: Product Focused, Client Focused, Membership Focused, and Event Focused.

🌀 You're familiar with the four types of entrepreneurs: Mission Based, Passion Based, Opportunity Based, and Undecided—and ideally have identified which one you are.

You've been filled in on the IN/UP/MAX model and how it applies to the progression of your business as it pertains to products and growth.

And finally, you now have a list of at least three Keyword Phrases that are representative of your business ideas. If you aren't sure you've got the Keyword Phrases right, don't worry; use what you have at this point. Learning and understanding what the framework is and how the process works are what matters. Think of it like finding the blueprint for validating every business idea you will ever have.

Progress Summary

You've just completed your Stage 1 in the Choose Method Process!

Here's a quick summary of your progress so far.

Stage 1—BRAINSTORM

☑ Step 1—Model Brainstorm

☑ Step 2—Market Brainstorm

☑ Step 3—Business Idea Brainstorm

STAGE 2—TEST

☐ Step 4—Bullseye Keyword

☐ Step 5—Market Size Sweet Spot

☐ Step 6—Market Competition Sweet Spot

☐ Step 7—Market Must-Haves

STAGE 3—CHOOSE

☐ Step 8—Choose Your Market

☐ Step 9—The Final Step to Launch

TEST

The name of the game is to stay in the game,
until you win the game.

Before you buy a car, you test drive it. Before you release software, you run a beta test. Before you jump in the pool, you test the water. Before you drink expired milk, you perform a smell test. You're not being overly controlling; you're being responsible. Practical. Vigilant. And that's exactly what you're doing here in Stage 2.

Results can be disastrous when you choose the wrong market, and the test process within the Choose Method will give you the confidence to move forward without feeling like you're risking everything: money (sometimes a lot of it), confidence (second-guessing yourself), or time (your most precious resource). Here in this stage, you can simply test an idea, and if it passes, great. If it doesn't, it is far better to know now before you go ahead and invest in it further. This stage was designed to give you the highest chance of achieving business success, and it contains one particular test that was one of *the* most significant eureka moments of my life. It demystifies one of *the* trickiest parts of choosing your market and transforms it from being a dark mystery to being crystal clear.

With the Brainstorming stage complete, here's what you're going to do as you make your way forward with your handful of business ideas: You'll get an official introduction to the Red light/Yellow light/Green light system as a way for you to gauge your progression. You'll quickly learn how effective it is in taking all the guesswork out of evaluating which of your brainstormed ideas are viable. It's an easy and clear indicator of whether or not your idea has passed each test and whether or not you should continue with it.

If you hit a Red light at any point through the test process, you'll go back to your brainstormed ideas and run another idea through. If you hit a Yellow light, you'll want to treat those ideas with caution. If you hit a Green light, you can move forward with assurance. And like I've said before, this is an iterative process, so it's normal to have to keep refining and going back through it until you've been given the Green light.

We'll use the traffic light approach to test your ideas against proven industry standards and assess their potential in three important areas. First, we're going to look at Market Size and figure out whether it's in the Sweet Spot for success (here's where I will share my eureka moment with you). It's both simple and profound, and you absolutely need it because you don't want a market that's too small, and believe it or not, you also don't want a market that's too big. And this test gives you a way to clearly determine which is which. Second, we'll look at Market Competition so you can be sure you don't have too many competitors, and also that you don't have too few competitors—or the biggest curse of them all, zero competitors. (Even though you might be tempted to think you've found a winner, little to no competition is actually a warning sign.) Finally, we'll be looking at your Market Must-Haves to see if your market has the five characteristics that will make your business idea sustainable for you, now and in the long term.

Testing in Stage 2 will give you peace of mind and clarity to make an informed decision about which market and business idea to embark on, and ultimately make it abundantly clear whether you're putting your boat in the right body of water. But in order to do this, you have to have something to test, right? And that something is your Bullseye Keyword.

STEP 4

Bullseye Keyword

In Step 3, your "I want to" statements produced *Keyword Phrases*. And constructing those sentences was a helpful exercise in figuring out the who and the what you want to focus on. Help real estate agents convert leads. Help teenagers acclimate to college. Help people paint their first watercolor painting. Indeed, each of these phrases is full of keywords!

But the *Bullseye Keyword* in Step 4 is a specific format for your business idea. It requires a pared-down version of your Keyword Phrases and, in the tests to come, will help you verify whether your idea has merit or not. The Bullseye Keyword is a short (generally one to three words) phrase that expresses the process or journey or transformation you're going to take people through. Let me reiterate the huge takeaway here: *your Bullseye Keyword must express the process or journey or transformation people will experience as a result of buying your product.*

Here's how to come up with your *Bullseye Keyword* candidates:

First, take the top three "I want to" statements that you came up with during the Brainstorm stage. Starting with your top contender, look at how you might express that Keyword Phrase (that is, everything that comes after

"I want to help people . . .") in the framework I just gave you: *a one- to three-word phrase that expresses the process or journey or transformation you're going to provide to people.*

For example, if my top business idea is "I want to help people care for their orchid," some Bullseye Keywords that follow the above framework might be "orchid care," "caring for orchids," "growing orchids," or "create orchid gardens." In the case of "orchid care," the word *care* represents the process or journey you can help people with in regard to their orchids. Sometimes the process or transformation is built into the keyword itself; for example, "home brewing" or "stroke recovery." And sometimes the process is baked into a one-word keyword like "mixology."

Perhaps a more digestible way to think about it is this: since selling *education and expertise* hinges on how-tos (more or less), think of these Bullseye Keywords as something you could teach someone. You can't teach how to "orchid" but you can teach "orchid care," "home brewing," and "mixology."

To have a successful business means providing customers with something of value, so when in doubt, ask yourself, "What do I want to help people do, achieve, experience, or have as an outcome related to my business idea?" This will ensure there's an active process or journey element to your answer.

If your "I want to" statement is "I want to help people brew their own beer," possible Bullseye Keywords could be "beer brewing," "home brewing," or "how to brew beer."

If your "I want to" statement is, "I want to help people recover from a stroke," Bullseye Keywords could be "stroke treatment," "post-stroke therapy," "stroke recovery," or "overcoming strokes."

Similar to the business idea brainstorm when the "I want to" statements were pretty straightforward in how they translated to a niche market, that can also be the case here. Bullseye Keywords can be incredibly obvious. Helping people manage their restaurants conjures up "restaurant management," or helping people design flower arrangements easily elicits "flower arranging." If it's not a straight shot, a common culprit is that your business idea isn't specific enough.

Remember Kristi Kennedy of Bee Friendly Now? While her son had severe autism and was struggling with bullying at school, behind the scenes, she and her other children were also experiencing varying degrees of abuse and bullying. She and her children found themselves in a delicate and transitional stage of life where hopelessness threatened to take over at any moment. Those struggles led to her initial business idea that revolved around the statement "I want to help people overcome obstacles in life."

That could have encompassed a great many things, not to mention made establishing a Bullseye Keyword quite difficult. As she started to sort through the specific process or journey of what her business idea could provide people, she leaned more and more toward a character- and leadership-based program that helped students with special needs enter a mainstream school environment.

She lived in Michigan at the time, so she went to the Michigan House of Representatives and Senate to seek support to pilot the program. The House chairman came back and asked if the program would help diminish bullying. Kristi felt that it would be a natural result of the program, but the more she thought about it, the more she realized that it was the ultimate output of what she wanted the program to offer. The longer she sat with the idea, the more it resonated.

It prompted her to shift her statement to "I want to help diminish bullying." It was specific enough to act as a North Star, general enough to include both the bully and the bullied, and flexible enough to offer scalable solutions. By shifting her primary focus, she shifted her statement, which led her to land on "stop bullying" as her Bullseye Keyword. Once she started testing it, she realized she was about to enter a viable niche market.

In this way, the Bullseye Keyword exercise can help you really home in on your idea.

To begin the process of defining your Bullseye Keyword, and to officially kick off the testing process, I have created the Choosing Your Green Light Market Worksheet to take you all the way through the Test stage. By the time you've completed it, you will have a very clear idea of what market to pursue, what business to start, and what niche to focus on. You will also have likely rejected or refined a number of your ideas, and I know I'm beating this into the ground, but that's a *good and normal part of the process*. Addition by subtraction—my favorite kind of math.

Perhaps more than any other worksheet featured in this book, I highly suggest you print the Choosing Your Green Light Market Worksheet from the Bonus Online Resource Area found at www.choosethebook .com/bonuses. It's an invaluable tool that will help you track your Bullseye Keywords as we move through the remaining steps of this journey, and is best utilized when you physically write and track your Bullseye Keywords as we go through each step.

For now, you'll just want to focus on Checkpoint 1 on the left-hand side of the worksheet and come up with a list of Bullseye Keyword Candidates for each of your top three business ideas. Start with your number-one priority. You might find multiple possible Bullseye Keywords for that business idea. List them all! Write each one on its own line in the space provided. Then move on to the next business idea and repeat until you've done that for your top three.

All set? Now you're going to do two very quick "first pass" tests here at Checkpoint 1 on your Worksheet for each of your Bullseye Keyword Candidates (we call these "first pass" tests because they give you a quick indication whether your Bullseye Keyword is potentially viable) via the aptly titled Google and Amazon tests.

Let's start with Google. This simply involves doing a Google search over at google.com and entering your Bullseye Keyword in the search bar and hitting enter. If the search results come back showing search results similar to the ones you have in mind, your Bullseye Keyword has passed, so you put a checkmark in the Google box next to that Bullseye Keyword.

An applicable example is one of my early business successes in the memory improvement niche. When I took that idea through this process, I had two potential Bullseye Keywords: "expand memory" and "improve memory."

When I applied the Google test to my first keyword, "expand memory," the first-page search results didn't align with what I thought I would see. Instead of being about how to remember more things and/or study for exams—which are the things I wanted to help people with—all the search results related to computer memory, like how to expand your RAM. In that case, I quickly knocked out the "expand memory" keyword. It had failed the first test.

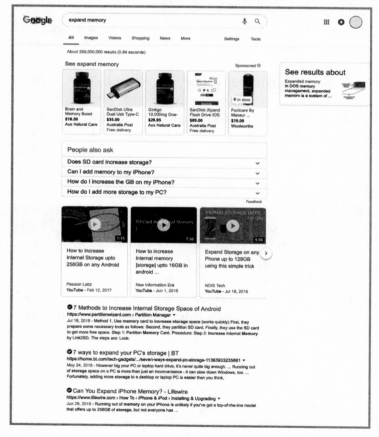

The first-pass Google test helps you see if your Keyword Phrase yields the first-page results you would expect. See this example where "expand memory" gave computer memory–related results instead of the hoped-for brain memory results.[1]

I moved on to "improve memory" and applied the Google test. All the search results on the first page were very much aligned with what I wanted to help people with—tips, exercises, articles, and products, all geared toward helping people remember what they wanted and ultimately achieve higher mental functioning. So that keyword got a checkmark and passed its first test.

When you get the right Keyword, your Google first-pass test will show first-page results that are aligned with what you expected to see. For example, "improve memory" reveals tips, exercises, and articles related to improving brain memory and recall.[2]

You can opt to make your way down the list and do the first-pass Google test for each of your proposed Bullseye Keywords, or, as soon as you get one that passes, you can move on to the Amazon test. The choice is yours. The only thing I have a firm opinion on is that you run this process through for all of your top three business ideas; don't just stop at your first one because it passed.

⊗ The Amazon first pass is very similar to the Google test, except now you go to amazon.com and enter your proposed Bullseye Keyword into the search bar. If the results of items listed for sale on the first page of Amazon's results come back as you might expect (that is, if products or information are related to how you want to help people), that keyword passes the Amazon test and gets a checkmark. If it doesn't get the expected results, that suggests your keyword is not an accurate or effective way to express your business idea. In that case, it fails and is knocked out of contention.

Looking at the "expand memory" versus "improve memory" example again, when I searched Amazon for "expand memory," I was presented with a range of computer equipment, memory cards, and memory sticks to buy. Not relevant. But when I searched for "improve memory," I got a mix of supplements and information geared toward helping people enhance their mental performance. Relevant.

Your Amazon first-pass test will also help you determine whether your keyword is relevant. For example, "expand memory" yields irrelevant computer equipment, memory cards, and memory sticks.

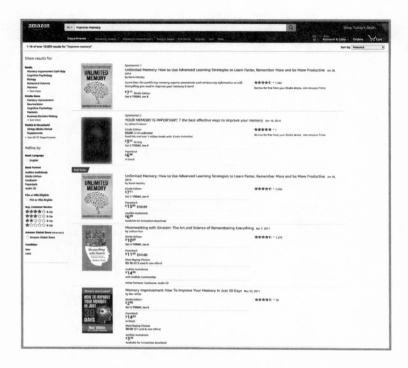

Compare that with the more relevant keyword "improve memory," which shows other educational material and resources to help increase comprehension and retention of information.

You may be wondering why I use Google and Amazon as the first line of defense in this exercise. Well, Google is the largest and most popular search engine in the world, so it gives you insight into what keywords the majority of people are searching for. Amazon is the world's largest online store, so it gives you insight into what keywords people are using to describe what they want to buy. By using this simple, trustworthy, and free strategy that very few people take full advantage of, you'll be able to quickly weed out which Bullseye Keywords should be eliminated from your list.

If you're still stuck on trying to land on the wording of your Bullseye Keywords, it may help to revisit the 25 profitable market niche ideas I shared previously in the Bonus Online Resource Area. On that list are actual keywords that passed the tests you're about to go through, and a quick review will reiterate the concise and active language that you'll want to land on.

The secret is to not underestimate the power of providing transformation for your consumers. It's not orchids; it's *growing* orchids or *caring for* orchids. It's not bees; it's bee*keeping*—you're teaching them the transformation of *keeping* bees. It's all about identifying what you're doing for the market and playing into the momentum, progress, and transformation that market success requires.

Ⓑ Continue running your Bullseye Keywords through the two first-pass tests via Google and Amazon that we mentioned earlier and note the outcomes in Checkpoint 1 on your Choosing Your Green Light Market Worksheet. The ones that successfully get two checkmarks will be the ones you'll take with you into the upcoming Sweet Spot tests. The first Sweet Spot test will be in regard to the ideal Market Size and the second relates to the ideal amount of Market Competition. For both, we're looking for markets that fit inside the Sweet Spot, both in terms of size and competition—so in other words, we're looking for markets that have a unique combination of being the right size and having the right amount of competition. When you find such a market, this is where things start to get interesting. You ready?

Market Size
Sweet Spot

At the beginning of this book I made a promise to you that I was going to demystify the process of what it takes to choose a successful market. And in Step 5, I am going to introduce you to one of *the* most crucial and clarifying concepts of the whole Choose Method: the Market Size Sweet Spot.

It is one of the single *biggest* discoveries I've made in my entire career. In fact, when I did the original research for it, it hardly seemed possible. Except that it is. I tested and retested. I've now seen it work in dozens of different markets, including my own and those of my most successful students and clients.

After many years and much trial and error, I figured out that there's a Sweet Spot for each market—and that Sweet Spot represents a Market Size that's not too big and not too small. Most believe the bigger the market, the better, but I'm about to debunk that myth.

If you put your boat in the middle of the ocean when you don't have the resources to expand your vessel into a larger ship suited to navigate big waters, you'll be swallowed up by the expanse, an irrelevant speck in a giant seascape. Conversely, if you put your boat in the middle of a still river, you can paddle as hard as you possibly can but there will simply not be enough volume to get you moving. They're equally problematic situations. An ocean-sized market is too large to enter. A still-river market is too small. The key is finding a Market Size in the middle between the vast ocean and the still river. The size of your market needs to be *just right*.

So how can you tell whether your market idea is inside the Market Size Sweet Spot or not? The answer has been hiding in plain sight for more than a decade, since Google released its free tool, Google Trends[1] in May 2006.

While it wasn't designed for this purpose, since its inception Google Trends has been gathering data and, as a by-product, creating a picture for business owners that will help them gain extraordinary insight into the size of market for *any* business idea under the sun. And now I have the *other* important piece of the puzzle: the exact location on the Google Trends graph of the Market Size Sweet Spot. This is a very tiny and very specific location on the Google Trends graph that, from my experience entering dozens of different markets, working with hundreds of clients over the past decade, and analyzing the graph location of the businesses that were successful and the ones that were not, is the exact range where your business idea has the greatest chance of success.

Importantly, this Market Size Sweet Spot works incredibly well if you are looking to build a six- or seven-figure business selling *education and expertise*. It doesn't necessarily apply if you're backed by millions of dollars in venture funding, if you're looking to build a *billion*-dollar company or sell cupcakes or widgets or become the next Nike, and I want to be up front with you about that.

I'm here to specifically help you grow your bootstrapped business selling *education and expertise* into a highly profitable and successful venture, and I'm pulling out all the stops to do it.

First, the basics: Here's how it works. Google Trends (https://trends.google.com) shows how often a particular search term is entered into Google relative to the total search volume across the world. That means, if there were 100 Google searches in total in the world right now, and 20 of them were for the words "build a LEGO® castle" and 10 of them were for "how to build a computer," then relatively speaking, there would be *twice* as many searches for "build a LEGO castle" compared to "how to build a computer." So it's a snapshot of how popular a particular search term is right now, compared to all the things people in the world are searching for.

This tool gives you a great benchmark of the popularity and relevance of your keyword. And while the actual number of searches for your keyword might go up and down, this *relative* benchmark is what we're going to focus on to show us where the Sweet Spot is in relation to your Market Size.

Once you go to Google Trends online, you'll see there are some search criteria you can enter to customize the results Google shows you. And you want to pay attention to two of these.

First, you'll see you can specify location. This is how you control how wide Google casts the net when looking at and displaying data on the number of searches being made on your specific keywords. Here you have some options. You can choose a particular country, which will only show you data on searches made within that country, or you can choose "Worldwide," which means

Google will show you data based on all searches around the globe. My recommendation is that you choose the "Worldwide" option, the reason being that one of the big benefits of selling *education and expertise* is that it gives you access to a global market, as opposed to having a small local business where you're limited by your local geography.

Second, you'll see you can nominate the timeframe. This determines how far back in time you want Google to look when displaying the search data. And my recommendation to you is that you choose the "Past 5 years" option. The reason to choose this is that you want to see how your keyword has performed not just over several months, but rather several years, so you can determine how longer-term trends relate and get a clearer picture of how stable or seasonal that keyword is. (We'll talk more about how you read the data later. For now I want to make sure you get the right data in the first place.)

Please assume that all the examples you see in this chapter from Google Trends are using these two settings. And I recommend that you do the same when you use Google Trends to help you choose *your* market.

For starters, we're going to use a practice keyword. First, go to Google Trends and enter the keyword "Pilates." After you press enter, you'll notice a graph is produced that shows the data results of consumer searches for that particular keyword. Now, go ahead and set your search criteria above the graph to "Worldwide" and "Past 5 years." Once the data refreshes, do you see how the blue line is pretty straight across?

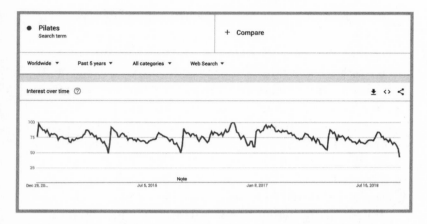

Using your practice keyword, "Pilates," you can see how the Google Trends search works (notice how the line is relatively horizontal, apart from a few seasonal highs and lows).

It's showing a somewhat stable market. There's a spike in January and a drop between Thanksgiving and Christmas each year, which is common for many health and wellness markets (here's looking at you, New Year's resolutions), and that alone implies that the market could be cyclical. This is an immediate clue! Think about what this could mean for your business. If your busy time at work is always in January, does that fit in with your lifestyle and your goals? It's also important to keep in mind that because cyclical markets go through highs and lows, they often have revenues to match.

But how does Pilates compare to other health-related niches? This is where Google Trends gets really interesting and really powerful because it enables you to quickly contrast your search with other keywords. Click the "+ Compare" at the top of the screen and enter an additional keyword, "keto." Now you see the Google Trends graph has *two* lines plotted on it. And you can see how Pilates and keto compare in terms of search volume. The new addition to the graph shows that the increasingly popular high-fat diet has similar cyclical spikes (which you can see with the spike occurring in the last 12 months on this chart). It's also important to note here that even though Pilates is more stable and, up until the most recent 12 months in this chart, bigger volume-wise, that doesn't necessarily mean it's in the Sweet Spot. Often the bigger markets are more competitive, more mature, and more expensive to enter.

What you *can* see from this graph is that search volume as measured by Google Trends *is* doing a great job of visualizing actual market behavior and popularity. Because unless you've been living under a rock, it's highly likely you noticed the big spike in popularity and interest in keto. Either you've tried it, or you have a friend who has tried it, or you've seen the explosion of keto-based information and products. A fact that is borne out in the Google Trends graph.

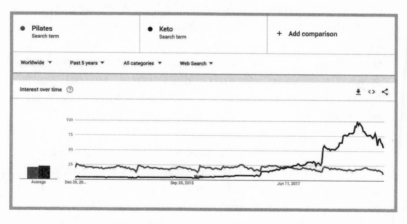

See how keywords compare. In this case, look at how "Pilates" compares with another health-related term, "keto." (Notice the big spike in search volume for "keto" in recent months.)

For the sake of comparisons, and to really test the theory that search volumes correlate with market size so that you can feel as confident in this tool as I do, let's measure Pilates against a market that garnered worldwide attention in a major and spectacular way.

Enter "bitcoin."

A very quick glance will show you that it had relatively similar keyword search volume to Pilates, with a massive one-time spike and sharp drop in 2017–18.

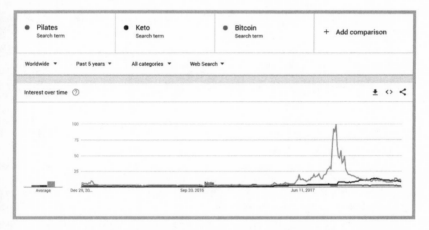

You can compare and contrast multiple keywords in one graph. See how our earlier graph changes when we add "bitcoin." (Notice how "Pilates" and "keto" are much smaller, relative to the big "bitcoin" spike in search volume.)

Importantly, that rise and fall in search volume corresponded with the massive rise and fall of bitcoin's share price around a similar timeframe. Again, you would have likely noticed this rapid influx of people to the bitcoin market during this time. It seemed you couldn't walk into a coffee shop or get in a taxi without hearing people talk about bitcoin. I remember one day even the person cutting my hair was talking about it!

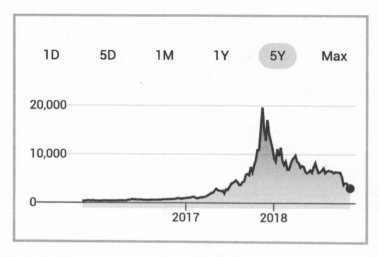

Interestingly, you can see how the spike in search volume for the keyword "bitcoin" seen in Google Trends corresponds with the spike in the share price—another indicator of the rapid influx of people to this market.[2]

Now do you get the gist of how this tool works? It provides a visual snapshot of how certain market niches might compare with others based on keyword search volume, and since that's precisely the type of information you need, it's a priceless tool.

How you determine whether the markets you're searching for are in the Market Size Sweet Spot comes down to whether your market falls within a specific range. But to properly understand how that range was established in the first place, let's go over some key characteristics that provide the parameters for the ideal Market Size.

First, you want markets that are stable or trending up. That signifies they have long-term potential. Current examples of stable or trending up markets over the past five years include markets like "renovation" and "online education," which have both been stable markets, and "social media," which is a consistent upward-trending market.

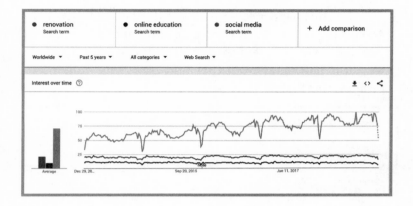

You want markets that are stable or trending up. That signifies they have long-term potential. Like the examples "renovation" and "online education" (stable) and "social media" (consistent upward trend).

Contrarily, the last thing you want to do is join a downward trending market, which usually happens when you hop on a fad bandwagon. Remember fidget spinners? Those came and went in a flash. As can be seen in the Google Trends graph for "fidget spinners" keyword search volume:

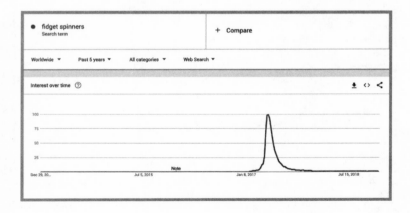

You don't want markets that are trending down or highly volatile, which often happens when you enter a fad market such as this example: "fidget spinners."

The same happened with a lot of the diets out there like "Atkins diet" or "paleo." They go in and out of fashion, and you don't want to catch them on the downswing. The risk to you is putting all your time and effort into building a business that basically disappears as your market disappears.

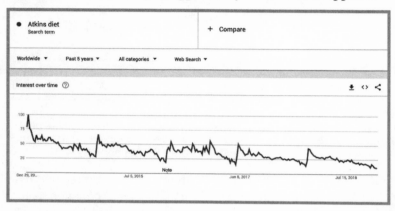

An example of a downward trending market for "Atkins diet" keyword.

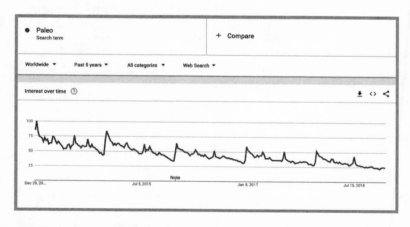

And another example of a downward trending market for "paleo" keyword. You want to avoid fad or downward-trending markets.

You will also want to find markets that satisfy your lifestyle. We touched on the cyclicality of a market like Pilates, and those types of markets are more common than you may realize. For example, the "carnations" market demonstrates powerful cyclicality.

Here's the Google Trends graph plotting the keyword search volume for "carnations" over five years.

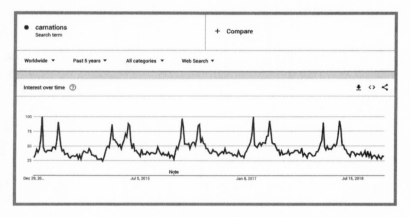

An example of a cyclical market, for keyword "carnations." Those two big spikes each year represent Valentine's Day and Mother's Day, peak periods of demand and interest.

See those two huge annual spikes fairly close to each other year after year? One in February and one in May. That's around Valentine's Day and Mother's Day, which is when, understandably, demand for carnations is highest. This demand is reflected in the search volume for the "carnations" keyword.

This graph shows you those would be your busiest times of the year if you're in the carnation business. If you don't want to work a lot in February or May, that is probably not a market you want to go into.

Now, those are all the foundation pieces. And on their own, they are definitely valuable as you go about deciding which market to choose. And if we stopped there, you'd already have some valuable ways to use Google Trends. But what I am about to show you now is a quantum level deeper and more powerful. When I first discovered it, I shared it with a colleague, and we just stared at the computer screen, speechless. I had found a key to open the window into a world that had *always* been there, waiting to be understood, but that had been locked away. It felt like we had discovered the *Rosetta stone* of Bullseye Keywords. But *this* Rosetta stone wasn't inscribed with a particular combination of ancient languages. Instead, it was inscribed with a particular combination of successful businesses to help you decode the billions of pieces of data available in Google Trends easily, and to almost instantly know, with confidence, whether *any* business idea you have is in the Market Size Sweet Spot I have identified—that is, the optimal sized market for six- and seven-figure *education and expertise* businesses to thrive. Not too narrow and not too broad. Just right.

The Rosetta Stone

The original Rosetta stone,[3] discovered in 1799, was a stone tablet inscribed in 196 BC on behalf of the Egyptian King Ptolemy V. The magnitude of this discovery was enormous because it contained the *same* decree in three different languages: The first, ancient Egyptian using hieroglyphic script; the second, ancient Egyptian using Demotic script; and the third, ancient Greek. Up until that time, the ancient Egyptian languages were lost to modern humanity. No one had been able to decipher all the texts being discovered on various Egyptian artifacts, architecture, and scrolls, severely limiting our understanding of the Ancient Egyptian world. The significance of the Rosetta stone is that while *no one* could understand ancient Egyptian languages, *many* scholars could understand ancient Greek. And because there are only minor differences between the three versions inscribed, the Rosetta stone became the *key* to deciphering Egyptian hieroglyphs, throwing open a window into ancient Egyptian history that had previously been closed, bringing the richness of the ancient Egyptian world to life.

The common thread of all the businesses in the Market Size Sweet Spot was a particular position on the Google Trends graph. I had found a very specific Market Size bandwidth that was a freakishly accurate predictor of success.

In fact, every single one of my 23 successful businesses fit in this narrow bandwidth. And when I tested the theory further by entering my *clients'* most successful businesses, they too fit in this tiny success window: the Market Size Sweet Spot. Then I tested my *students'* most successful business and they *also* fit in this Sweet Spot! And here's the kicker: Those businesses that I had never quite been able to make work, or that had failed miserably? Not *one* of them was in this Sweet Spot.

The phrase "secret to success" is so overused, but this truly is one of *the* single *biggest* discoveries I have ever made, and it's given me a window onto success unlike anything else. And up until now I've only shared it with my inner circle of colleagues, clients, and students. But I've decided I'm going to reveal it to a much wider audience in the pages of this book, for the first time ever.

Here's what I mean.

The Market Size Sweet Spot is a narrow bandwidth in which markets are the ideal size for *education and expertise* businesses to thrive. Identifying exactly what this range is has taken me years to figure out and demystify. Over the following pages, I'm going to show you the markets that my students, my clients, and I have had the most success in and *exactly* where that Sweet Spot is and how you can use Google Trends to measure it within seconds and test your own market ideas to see if they also fall within that *same* Market Size Sweet Spot.

Let's start with "orchid care," my trusty ol' example. If you enter that into the Google Trends search bar, you'll see that it's a relatively stable market overall. There are small spikes around Valentine's Day and Mother's Day each year (similar to "carnations" but not nearly as extreme). Seeing those spikes will immediately tell you when the biggest times of the year will be—which is helpful to know for your own personal schedule *and* for preparing promotions and sales and gearing up in terms of team and other resources.

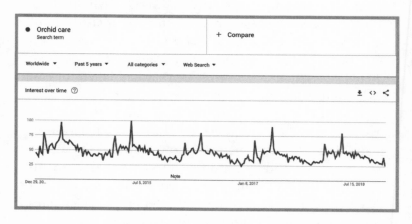

The "orchid care" keyword example represents one of my own proven successful businesses. Note that it's relatively stable with some peaks around Valentine's and Mother's Day (like the "carnations" keyword).

Now compare the "orchid care" example with "improve memory" using "+Compare" in Google Trends. Do you see how that keyword is in the same vicinity of search volume (that is, it's at about the same level on the graph) as "orchid care"?

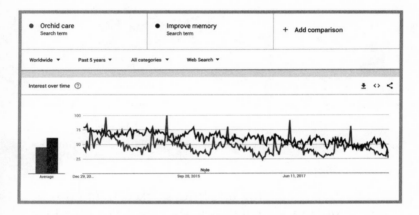

Now compare "orchid care" with the keyword from another one of my successful businesses, "improve memory," and notice that it also has a similar search volume.

Next, I want to include a market from one of our highly successful ASK Method clients, *New York Times* best-selling author and creator of Platform University Michael Hyatt, who serves the leadership skills market. If you enter the "leadership skills" keyword into that same graph now (using "+Compare"), you'll see it's a little larger but also in a similar keyword search volume range.

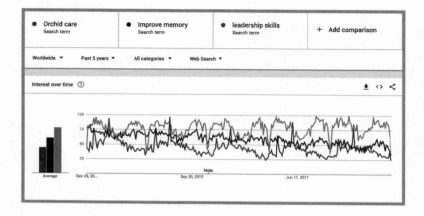

When you add the keyword "leadership skills" from one of my client's successful businesses and compare it with "orchid care" and "improve memory," you'll see it's a little larger but also in a similar keyword search volume range.

So those are highly successful markets from my own businesses and a client's business. Now let's take a look at a long-proven success story from a student's market. Sean Bissell was one of the first students to have massive success with the ASK Method. He's an Opportunity Based entrepreneur, and after a brainstorming session together, I helped him arrive at the Beekeeping market. Again, that keyword falls into a search volume range that is very similar to the other businesses I just mentioned. Go ahead and add the "beekeeping" keyword into the same Google Trends graph now (using "+Compare") and you'll see:

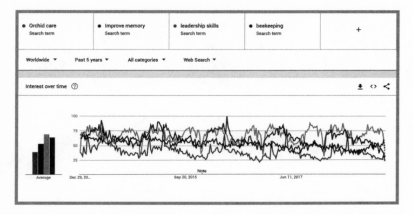

Now take a look at what happens when you add the "beekeeping" keyword from one of my students' successful businesses to the mix of already successful businesses, and check out the similarities in terms of their position on the graph. Eureka! Our Rosetta stone.

When I entered dozens and dozens of other successful business keywords, they all fell within this same range. The keywords listed here became our Rosetta Stone Keywords. That means you could enter these four keywords ("orchid care," "improve memory," "leadership skills," "beekeeping") into Google Trends at any time and, using the [+Compare] option, add a fifth keyword (*any* keyword) to see if it *also* lands inside this Market Size Sweet Spot Range, or if it lands outside of it. The *reason* for these four keywords in particular is that they represent not only the middle of the Sweet Spot range, but also the upper and lower ends of it as well.

Let me illustrate just how incredibly powerful this combination of the Google Trends tool with the Rosetta Stone Bullseye Keywords is when evaluating which market to go into.

For this next example, I'm going to draw on the experience of my client Ron Reich, whom I mentioned earlier. When Ron first came to me, we embarked on a brainstorm session together and he immediately headed toward the self-help space when thinking about which market he might like to go into.

If you look at "self help" in Google Trends when compared with the Rosetta Stone Bullseye Keywords, it's immediately apparent just what a giant market it is:

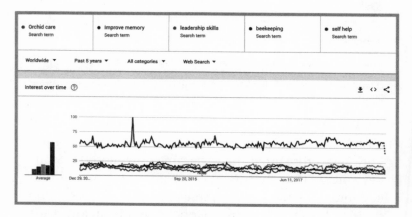

When you look at the "self help" keyword in Google Trends when with the other Rosetta Stone Bullseye Keywords, you can immediately see that it's a much bigger market.

This graph shows Self Help is a huge and daunting market that could prove to be too big and broad to make any progress in, or too vast and dangerous to survive in.

So we looked at other smaller niches within that larger Self-Help market, like "improve confidence" and "be more productive," and they tended to be too small.

Take a look for yourself in Google Trends now.

See how each of the search volumes for these terms are way below the Market Size Sweet Spot Range that the Rosetta Stone Bullseye Keywords are in?

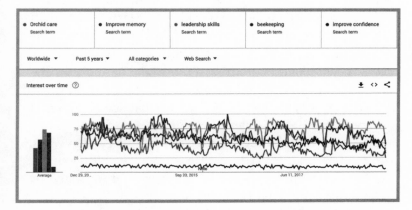

See how the search volume for the "improve confidence" keyword (an alternative to "self help") is just too small, located way below the range that the Rosetta Stone Bullseye Keywords are in?

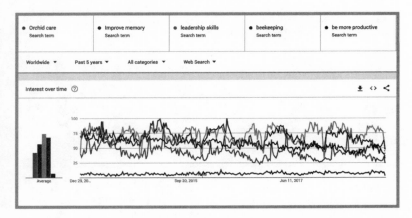

Same for the "be more productive" keyword. It's way below the Market Size Sweet Spot indicated by the other Rosetta Stone Bullseye Keywords, implying the market is likely too small.

Ron and I then started to brainstorm ideas in a completely different area—the dog market. Because that's so general, it also proved to be far too massive. For example, we started by looking at the keyword "dog training," but we found that it was *way* outside the Market Size Sweet Spot. So I helped him niche it down even further. We thought, well, if dog training is too broad, perhaps there is a specific *kind* of training that might be more in the Sweet Spot. And maybe we don't want to focus on training for *every* type of dog, but rather a particular subset of dogs. Through this hugely helpful process, we ultimately settled on "potty train puppy" as his Bullseye Keyword. If you type that into Google Trends now, you'll see that it falls just within the Market Size Sweet Spot indicated by the Rosetta Stone Bullseye Keywords.

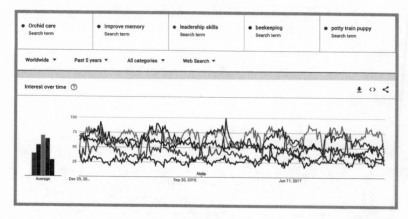

While our first ideas were outside the Market Size Sweet Spot, we found a strong contender by niching down in the dog care market to the keyword "potty train puppy."

Are you starting to see that there may be something to the markets that fit in this particular range? They're not too broad and they're not too narrow.

They are *just* right.

If you compare any of the examples I just gave you with the Pilates example from earlier, you'll see just how broad Pilates is. It's *way* outside the Sweet Spot range, proving it's too large, too competitive, and something you'd want to consider niching down.

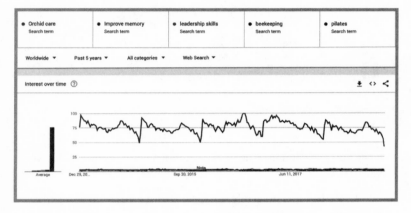

This graph shows you the previous Rosetta Stone Keywords ("orchid care," "improve memory," "leadership skills," and "beekeeping") compared with the earlier "Pilates" example, which is way outside the Market Size Sweet Spot (indicating you would need to consider niching down).

That said, you have to be careful not to go too far in the opposite direction and niche down too narrowly. Take "Pilates ball exercises," for example. When compared to the Rosetta Stone Bullseye Keywords, you can see just how miniscule some niche markets go. That's way too small!

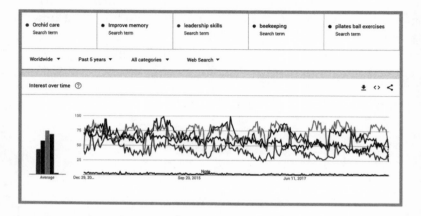

While niching down markets like "Pilates" that are too big, it is important to be careful not to go too far in the opposite direction and niche too narrowly (for example, as you can see in this graph, "Pilates ball exercises" is too small).

Let's bring the Red, Green, and Yellow traffic lights into this now. What you've essentially been seeing with these last few examples is the keywords that fit *within* the same range as the Rosetta Stone Bullseye Keywords (e.g., "potty train puppy") are Green light markets that mean "Yes, go!" And keywords that are *outside* the range of the Rosetta Stone Bullseye Keywords (e.g., "self help," "dog training," "Pilates," "be more productive," and "Pilates ball exercises") are Red light markets that mean "No, stop!" And then there are *some* markets that may be mostly outside the Market Size Sweet Spot but that are just touching some of the Rosetta Stone Bullseye Keyword graphs on the outer edge of the range. These are Yellow light markets that mean "Proceed with caution."

Here's an example that shows you all three traffic lights as they might appear during the process of deciding on your own Green light market.

Let's say I wanted to expand into a new market to supplement my Orchid Care business. And I was hoping to find something that was in the gardening space that perhaps my existing customers might be interested in. So, I Brainstorm and then Test the following Bullseye Keywords: "African violet care," "rose care," "cactus care," and "hydroponics."

When you look at the Google Trends graphs for each of these keywords side by side, compared with the Rosetta Stone Bullseye Keywords, you can see that African violet care is way below the Market Size Sweet Spot Range and therefore too small (Red light) and Hydroponics is way above the Market Size Sweet Spot Range, therefore too big (*another* Red light). Cactus care is mostly below the Sweet Spot and therefore likely too small, *although* it *does* touch the Sweet Spot Range in a couple of places, making this one a borderline keyword (Yellow light). And then there's rose care, which is smack bang in the middle of the Sweet Spot Range and represents another likely successful market opportunity (Green light).

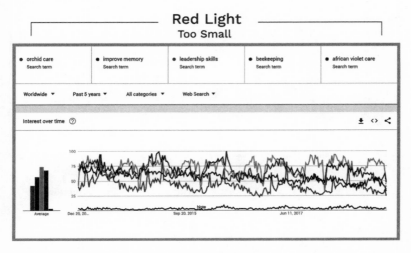

Red light gardening-related keywords outside the Market Size Sweet Spot: "African violet care" (too small) and "hydroponics" (too big).

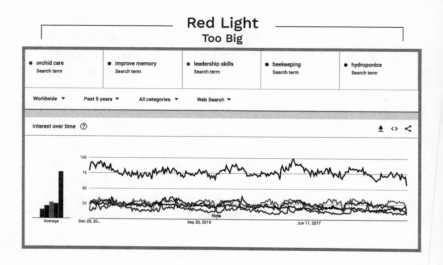

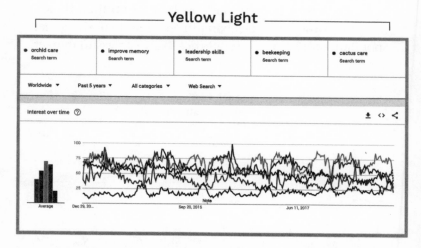

Yellow light gardening-related keywords on the Market Size Sweet Spot borderline: "cactus care" (mostly outside but touching the Rosetta Stone range).

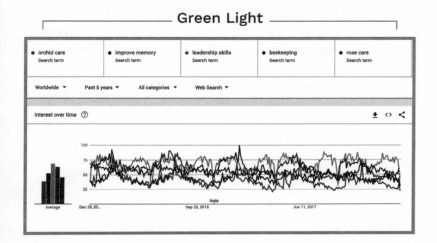

Green light gardening-related keywords right in the middle of the Market Size Sweet Spot: "rose care" (right in line with the Rosetta Stone Keywords).

Now it's your turn to see if *your* Bullseye Keywords are in the Market Size Sweet Spot. Head back to the Choosing Your Green Light Market Worksheet Checkpoint 1, where you listed all your Bullseye Keywords. Now take all the Keywords that already passed both the Google and Amazon first-pass tests and do the Market Size Sweet Spot Test by comparing each keyword with the Rosetta Stone Bullseye Keywords: "orchid care," "improve memory," "leadership skills," "beekeeping." Now you will be able to see *instantly* whether they fall within the Market Size Sweet Spot or not.

Remember: If the Google Trends graph for your Bullseye Keyword is completely inside the Market Size Sweet Spot Range, it's a Green light and you can move forward. If the graph is clearly outside the Market Size Sweet Spot Range—either too big or too small and not touching any part of the Rosetta Stone Bullseye

Keywords—it's a Red light, which means stop, don't move forward. If your keyword is partially touching or partially inside or outside the Market Size Sweet Spot Range, it's a Yellow light and you can keep it on your list for now; this is one you may decide to pause or move forward on when it comes to the next step in the Test process.

But what happens if you discover that your very favorite business idea is outside the Sweet Spot? Does that mean it's destined to fail? No. If your Bullseye Keyword doesn't fit within range at first, it doesn't necessarily mean there's no hope for your business idea or niche. It might simply mean you need to go through a process of refining your Bullseye Keyword further to really find the ideal Sweet Spot. That could mean that you niche it down to make your market idea more specific, like Ron Reich did, or that you need to go broader to make your market idea serve a bigger audience. This Market Size Sweet Spot test is meant to help you reframe the focus of your business, so it might just be that you haven't yet zeroed in on the ideal way to frame and focus your market. That's why this is such an incredibly valuable process!

You now have a quantifiable, *easy* way to instantly evaluate your business ideas and become clear and confident about your niche.

Really, *anyone* can do this.

Does that mean you will get it right the first time? No.

Does that mean that you won't have times when it feels hard? No.

Does that mean you might not have to make some unexpected pivots along the way? No.

Take ASK Method student Anna Baumgartner, for example. Anna participated in a live Choose Your Market training that I conducted, which included a 10-day Choose Your Market Challenge.

During those 10 days, Anna documented the process and her discoveries along the way in real time. She shared how she went from knowing nothing about the Choose Method to finding *her* Green light market (spoiler: it was not the market she expected, and it was not without some Red lights and obstacles along the way, but it still worked out wonderfully for her!).

Here's a quick summary in Anna's *own words*:

Day 0—Introduce Yourself

I teach entrepreneurs how to hire and manage their VA (virtual assistant). My goal: I would like to confirm the niche market I'm in (VA), and I'd also like to learn more about Ryan's process for choosing a market.

Day 1—Brainstorm Your Business Model

I choose the *education and expertise* business model because that's where most of my experience is. I enjoy sharing knowledge and ideas with others in a creative but practical way so that they can immediately apply it, and it makes good business sense due to the high number of people spending more to access online learning. In terms of products, I would consider online courses, coaching/consulting, webinars, and events.

Day 2—Brainstorm: What Type of Entrepreneur Are You?

I'd say I naturally tend toward Mission Driven, but lately I'm more open to opportunities that present themselves to me. I love to serve adults who want to improve their lives. The more my clients are involved and excited, the better my coaching becomes. It really helps if they feel they need what I have to offer.

Considering my expertise and passions, there are a few different kinds of people I can help, and here are the major ones: entrepreneurs who want to learn to manage their small teams or VA teams, people who want to be able to function in the Chinese language, and parents who need to know how to help their kids who have fallen out of love with math.

Day 3—Brainstorm Your Business Ideas

My top three business ideas: I want to help people to 1) Manage their VAs 2) increase the quality of elder care 3) learn to read music through games.

Day 4—Test Your Bullseye Keywords

The Bullseye Keywords that passed the Google and Amazon tests for my top three "I want to" statements are: "read music," "train a virtual assistant," "elderly care tips." I used thesaurus.com to find new possible Bullseye Keywords because the first few I tried didn't pass the tests and it worked—thanks for that tip, Ryan! This helped me realize the importance of not going with what words I think of but rather what the people who are searching are thinking of.

Day 5—Test Your Market Size Sweet Spot

Only one of my Bullseye Keywords that passed the Google and Amazon tests was a Green light—"read music." "Train a virtual assistant" and "elderly care tips" were so low they didn't even register, so I gave them a Red light.

Note: Here at Day 5, we've covered the steps in the process that I have taught you so far. I will share more on the process from here throughout the rest of this book, but I wanted to give you a preview of what's ahead via Anna's summary.

Day 6—Test Your Market Competition Sweet Spot

Today was definitely full of emotions! But it's all good! Market Competition Sweet Spot tests: I was starting to get psyched after completing Days 1 to 5 led me to consider choosing the Bullseye Keywords "reading music." Until I discovered in this step that it was a Red light! So I circled back to the beginning, looking through my brainstorms from Day 1, and started testing my 4th and 5th choices. I was really surprised in working through the steps to find that "learn Chinese" keyword is a Green light. So without going through each step in this process, I probably would not have considered this market. Thanks to Ryan for being real with us in talking about the emotions that go along with the process of choosing your market!

Day 7—Test the Market Must-Haves

My Bullseye Keyword "learn Chinese" is Green!

Day 8—IN, UP, MAX One-Page Business Model

I've mapped out my IN, UP, and MAX product ideas!

Day 9 Challenge—Choose Your Market

I only had one Green light market, which is "learn Chinese." The rest are Red light.

Day 10—Next Steps

For the "learn Chinese" idea, I will find out what my ideal customer thinks, wants, and needs using the ASK Method. I'll start by coming up with a "Single Most Important Question," which I'll ask and get feedback on. Something like "When it comes to learning Chinese, what's your single biggest challenge?" I'd also like to know whether people are most interested in learning Chinese for doing business, for work, for travel, or just because it's cool, ha ha. Woohoo! I made it through to Day 10 of the challenge and most importantly, discovered that I had been in a Red light market! So glad to have found out before I went any further. I feel more confident now that I've chosen a Green light market.

The best part about Anna's Choose Method journey? She is now building a business in the Learn Chinese market, but it took the Choose Method to help her see it. Plus, she successfully avoided wasting further time in the Red light market she was in when she started this process.

And here's the cherry on top: both her son and her daughter are helping her in the Learn Chinese business! Anna said this was a totally unexpected result of choosing the right market for her.

Anna's story is proof that once you take the time to really get clear on your Bullseye Keywords and are prepared to go back over the process a few times until you find your Green light market, you really can create the business and life you dream of.

To that end, let's revisit the "orchid care" example, which is one of our Rosetta Stone Bullseye Keywords. If I had thought I was in the orchid business—meaning, if I had framed my business idea as being about "orchids," it would not have been in the Market Size Sweet Spot and I would have walked away from an awesome business opportunity. If you look up the term "orchids" in Google Trends, you'll see it's far too broad. And that's because people searching for orchids aren't necessarily searching for information about how to *care* for their orchids, which is what I wanted to sell.

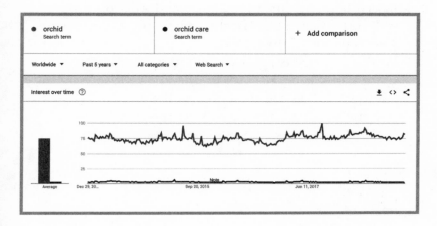

Green light gardening-related keywords right in the middle of the Market Taking time to refine your Bullseye Keyword makes all the difference. Compare "orchids" (very far outside the Market Size Sweet Spot) with "orchid care" (a proven and successful business idea inside the Market Size Sweet Spot).

Instead, consumers might be looking to buy actual orchid flowers or purchase special fertilizers or pots. They could be trying to find an orchid club or get photos of orchids, or studying up for their school project on orchids. None of that aligned with what I was trying to provide them. I'm not in the orchid business; I'm in the orchid *care* business. There's a big difference. This is a lesson both in the importance of Bullseye Keywords and in not rejecting potentially valid ideas just because they fall short the first time through Google Trends. Sometimes you just need to find your edge.

🐝 It's possible that your idea has great potential. Use this testing process as an opportunity to sharpen, clarify, and hone that idea accordingly. After running all your ideas through Google Trends, you'll want to move forward with your shortlist of Bullseye Keywords that passed both the first-pass Google and Amazon tests, as well as the Market Size Sweet Spot test. This brings you to Checkpoint 2 on the Choosing Your Green Light Market Worksheet. At this point you will transfer your shortlist of successful keywords over to Checkpoint 2, so you can see whether they are going to pass the other Sweet Spot test: the Market Competition Sweet Spot.

Market Competition Sweet Spot

In the competitive world that so many of us live in, a common misconception is that we must eliminate the competition in *business* in order to be successful; to be the best means to be the only one standing. Yet I'm here to tell you that when it comes to choosing your market, you actually want competition. Similar to the Market Size Sweet Spot, the secret here is having the *right number* of competitors. Not too many, but not too few.

I think the biggest fear around competition in the business world is that there are too many people competing for the same clients. The worry is that the bigger, more established players have an unfair advantage in scooping up all the leads and that businesses with bigger budgets, bigger teams, and more resources force up the price of advertising, which means the smaller folks can't compete in that same market.

First, I'll validate the small portion of the mindset that's actually true. If you have too much competition, it might imply your market is already oversaturated or so mature that it could be hard or expensive to gain traction within it. Quite frankly, it could be a bloodbath of people always reducing prices and climbing all over each other to get the sale. (It's what *Blue Ocean Strategy* authors W. Chan Kim and Renée Mauborgne call a "red ocean" for that very reason.) It can often take a very long time before you get a return on investment, or it may just be downright unprofitable.

On the other end of the scale, some people think that finding a market with no or too little competition is seen as a plus. They think they'll have the market to themselves and get to monopolize the need, but very likely, there's a reason no one is in the market. There's not really a big need. Not enough competition is just as problematic as having too much. Net: take the lack of competition as a definitive warning sign.

In the quest for originality, some people think they've missed an opportunity if someone has already done it or created it and that creating a successful business means coming up with a brand new idea that will blow everyone's minds with something the world has never seen.

I'm all about filling holes that need to be filled, but here's the truth of the matter: *pioneers get shot and settlers get rich.*

You don't have to be the first one in a market forging the way. Yes, the early pioneers had the greater opportunity to stake a claim, but they also had greater risks. Once they found gold, oil, or water, it was all too easy for someone to set up shop right next to them and tap into the same source from an adjoining field with none of the risk or cost associated with the pioneers' venture.

You want to be like the settlers who came in after the pioneers had carved a trail and done all the hard, dangerous work. The settlers were able to learn from where the pioneers failed and where they thrived. They fast-tracked their results for a lot less risk and expense.

Google wasn't the first search engine. They identified an opportunity that someone else pioneered, built a better mousetrap, and settled in that space.

Similarly, Facebook wasn't the first social network.

Amazon wasn't the first online bookseller.

Apple wasn't the first to sell smartphones or MP3 players.

They all simply found something that was working, that someone else had pioneered, and made it better. And that's exactly how you should be thinking: You want to be looking for a market with *competitors who are succeeding in spite of themselves.* That is, evidence that they're making money, in spite of having holes or gaps or something they're missing that represents an opportunity for you. This is what I found in the Scrabble tile jewelry market—I couldn't believe how much money someone could be making with such a poorly created product. Gone are the days of assuming you have to monopolize a market in order to be successful; the reality is that you're looking to build something just a little bit better or a little bit different where there's already a preexisting demand and evidence of preexisting success, so that you have an existing market to sell to.

So, how do you find out whether your idea fits in the Market Competition Sweet Spot? In a word, advertising. But your competitors', not yours.

You see, if you look around your proposed market and notice that competitors within the space are spending money on marketing, your future is looking bright. Here's why: marketing costs money, so if competitors are using paid advertising to promote their products or services, that means they're making enough of a profit to be able to afford the marketing. Nobody will spend money on paid ads for any extended period of time if they're not making money. It's not a perfect indicator, but it is a good marker to show you that the market you're thinking of entering is viable.

Remember Sean Bissell and the success he found in the beekeeping market? Years ago, Sean was working a job doing search engine optimization (SEO) for a marketing company when he decided to start his own business. The only problem was he didn't feel like he had any expertise (aside from doing SEO for other people), so he simultaneously worked on brainstorming a business idea while trying to find an expert to partner with.

His exploration ultimately led to the testing of two niche market options: one was the hummingbird market, and the other was beekeeping. They seemed like very similar markets on the surface—they're both small species with buzzing wings, and people make a hobby out of attracting them—but when Sean really did the research, he found one enormous difference. The hummingbird market had absolutely no competition in terms of advertising online, but the beekeeping market did. The perfect amount, in fact. The Sweet Spot.

How did he figure it out? A simple test. Whereas for the Market Size Sweet Spot we used Google Trends to see *what* people were searching for, now we want to see how many people are *advertising* online on your Bullseye Keyword to gauge the level of competition. And to do this, we shift our attention from Google to Amazon. Why we focus on Amazon specifically is because while people go to Google to search for information, people go to Amazon to spend *money. To* look at your competition, we want to look where the *buyers* are. In fact, in 2018, Amazon accounted for 49 percent of all online retail spending in the United States.[1] In other words, $0.49 of every dollar spent online in the U.S. was spent at Amazon.com.

When you visit Amazon, if you can see businesses not only *selling* their books, programs, and products there but also spending money to *advertise* those same products, it tells you that those businesses are finding it worthwhile to spend money on that advertising. In other words, they're making a return on their investment. Just because someone has a book for sale on Amazon, that doesn't mean they're necessarily making any meaningful profit from that book. But if they're *spending* money to also *advertise* that book on Amazon, chances are very strong that they are actually *making* money from it in their business.

Now, importantly, you're not looking for just any advertising. You're specifically looking for evidence of competitors on Amazon who are selling *education and expertise* because that's what you'll presumably be selling. It is also important to note that Amazon has a bias toward physical, non-information products, so it's possible you'll find lots of ads for non-information products matching your keyword search. You want to make it a point to look for ads selling *education and expertise*: books, Kindle e-books, resource guides, and so on.

Gauge the level of competition in the market for your keyword by looking at the number of other businesses paying for ads promoting related *education and expertise* products and services on Amazon (for example "improve memory").

> NOTE: The Amazon screenshots throughout the book represent only a partial view of each page. To get the full count of advertisers, you'll need to scroll through the entire first page on your own device for each of your keyword searches.

The way you're going to analyze this test is to tally up the number of the advertisers using your Bullseye Keyword who appear on page 1 of Amazon. You can tell which product listing on Amazon is a paid advertisement because Amazon indicates it is a "sponsored" listing. Amazon changes its page layouts on a weekly and sometimes daily basis, constantly testing new page formats and design. And remember: the results are *dynamic*. So what you see today will likely be different tomorrow, and you may need to look around a bit to find those sponsored listings. Start at the very top of the page, search at the very bottom, and be sure to look closely right in the middle of the page, where sponsored listings are sometimes tucked right between multiple non-sponsored listings.

The step-by-step process is as follows: First, on a full desktop or laptop browser, go to http://www.amazon .com. (If you're outside the U.S., you'll want to go to the .com site specifically, as opposed to, for example, your localized .ca .uk or .au version of the site. Unlike Google Trends, which gives us the option to look at worldwide results, Amazon localizes its website by region and by country. Since it's the largest consumer market in the world, we use the U.S. market as a worldwide proxy.) Second, type into the search bar your first shortlisted Bullseye Keyword and hit enter. Third, do a scan on the page for "Sponsored Listing" and make a note of the number of products selling *education and expertise* in some way on that first page of results that are sponsored listings.

🕑 Once you've done that, head back to the Choosing Your Green Light Market Worksheet, where you have added your shortlist of Bullseye Keywords to Checkpoint 2. If there are between three and seven "Sponsored Posts" or advertisers on page 1 of Amazon using your Bullseye Keyword, mark it as a Green light. If there are 1 to 2 or 8 to 9, mark it as a Yellow light. And if there are zero, or 10 or more, mark it as a Red light. This breakdown correlates to you looking for the right number—not too many but not too few. And remember: you're only looking at the first page and only tallying the competitors who are advertising an *education or expertise-related* product.[2]

Like the Google Trends Rosetta stone, these ranges are based on my three-year quest to reverse engineer both my own most successful markets compared to the ones in which I failed or struggled, as well as the most successful markets of my students and clients compared to those that didn't work out.

After I analyzed hundreds of different markets, the trends and cutoffs became clear. On more than one occasion, this process was painful for me, because I discovered more than one market I went into that failed would've been a clear Red light at this stage of the process. In fact, later in this chapter I'll share with you one of the most expensive and frankly embarrassing failures early on in my career. It's a market that the Competition Sweet Spot test would have flagged as a clear Red light. I just didn't have the experience or wisdom at the time to know I should've pivoted into a different direction. I'll also share with you a few of the markets I *did* steer away from after learning the importance of this test, and how I dodged a few proverbial bullets along the way . . .

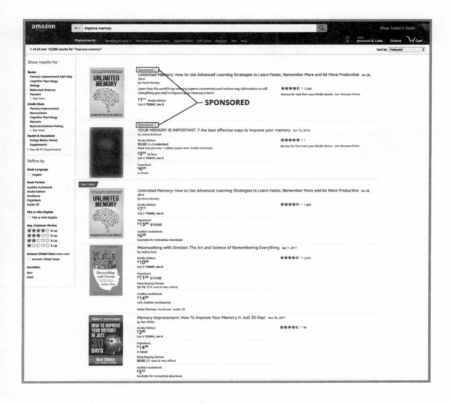

Look for the sponsored posts and other paid advertising featured on page 1 of Amazon search results for your keyword. In this case "improve memory" had six sponsored listings featuring products selling *education and expertise*, putting it in the Market Competition Sweet Spot.

So, looking at each of *your* potential Bullseye Keywords and plugging them into Amazon, what are your results?

If you're like most people, you may start to discover that similarly sized markets from the Google Trends Market Size Sweet Spot test have radically different levels of competition based on the Amazon Competition test.

Here's a sampling of some results that my clients and students have had in going through this same process:

"Home brewing": There were multiple people advertising, but every single one of them was selling some kind of physical equipment or home brewing kit along with education in the form of a guide or training. If you were open to selling physical equipment bundled with your information, it'd be a Green light. If not, it's a Red light.

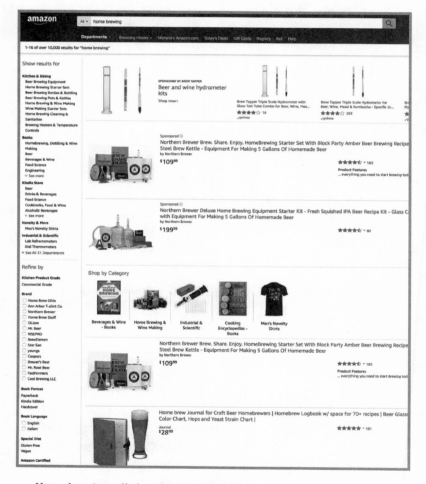

Home brewing: all the advertisers were promoting physical equipment or home brewing kits along with information. If you were open to selling physical equipment bundled with your information, it'd be a Green light. If not, it's a Red light.

"Learn to code": There were eight people advertising books and other information products on the topic of learning to code. So, while "learn to code" was a Green light on the Google Trends Market Size Sweet Spot test, it's a Yellow light here on the Amazon Market Competition Sweet Spot test.

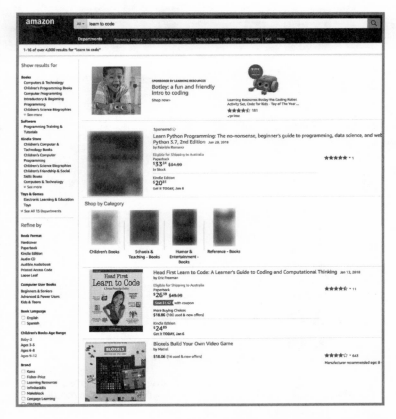

While "learn to code" was a Green light on the Google Trends Market Size Sweet Spot test, it's a Yellow light here on the Amazon Market Competition Sweet Spot test. NOTE: You can't see it here on this extract but the full Amazon page one search results featured 9 sponsored listings, which made it a Yellow light.

"Presentation skills": There were five different advertisers. That's a sign they're making money. Each one was a product selling *education and expertise,* so it got a Green light.

"Presentation skills" got a Green light because there were five different advertisers selling *education and expertise* on page 1 of Amazon test results.

This process will likely further refine your keywords, and by now you might have already had to go back to the drawing board a few times as your keywords hit Red lights. I've hit my fair share. There were the quinceañera market, my grand idea to go into flea removal (spoiler alert: yeah, that didn't work out), scrapbooking bargains (don't ask), daily cartoons geared for crafters (trust me, I wish I was joking), and Oriental art boxes using leftover origami paper (yep, I'm serious). In all of these instances, the competition was either way too extreme or practically nonexistent (or the idea was just horrible), so I didn't proceed.

Some of my worst ideas included "scrapbooking bargains," a market where no one was paying for *any* ads on Amazon (I wish I'd known at the time that was a sign it was a Red light market).

There are also repercussions to proceeding with a business idea despite too much or too little competition. I've had my fair share of those too. One of my biggest failures early in my career was in pest control. There were a few massive companies that were the big-money players in the space, and then a bunch of one-person operators who had to split the rest of the pie.

I decided to pursue that market without the benefit of the experience I have today, and without the process and framework outlined in this book. If my Choose Method had existed back then, it would have led to the discovery right from the start that the pest control market was a Red light market. That knowledge would have saved me from making a $75,000 mistake and losing nearly a year of my life trying to pursue it. To this day, it was one of the most expensive lessons of my career.

And before I landed on orchid care, I was looking at the orchid market in general (more along the lines of selling orchids), and I saw we would be eaten alive if we tried to go up against 1-800-Flowers or other huge brands that had a ton of money. It brings up a valuable lesson: go after what you can feasibly accomplish, and don't go after what you can't. Bill Gates might be able to solve the worldwide problem of malaria, but you likely can't. And that's okay!

Billion-dollar problems require billion-dollar budgets. What kind of budget do you have? When I first got started with a small budget, the first problem I tried solving was also small: how to build Scrabble tile jewelry. Not how to cure world hunger. From there, I was able to grow into bigger markets and solve bigger problems. The big lesson here: start where you can.

When Dr. Beverly Yates became an ASK Method Business Coaching client, she was a naturopathic physician with her own practice in San Francisco. While a part of her was content, she wanted to progressively build a business that didn't tie her to a physical practice. Was there a way she could use her expertise to impact patients all around the world?

As soon as she started brainstorming, she kept noticing that many of the women who came to see her were frustrated in their attempts to lose weight. Dr. Yates knew (as I'm sure you do too) that the weight loss market is overly saturated with huge competitors. She accepted the fact that she couldn't compete with the bigwigs but still wondered if she could have a presence in a related niche market.

Together we looked at all the different types of weight loss situations and kept running into two subgroups of women who came up over and over again as candidates for a potential market. One was HCG injections, which are a hormone-based treatment available by prescription that women can administer themselves. The other was weight gain associated with PCOS (polycystic ovary syndrome). The Amazon test revealed that the Bullseye Keyword "PCOS diet" fell into the Market Competition Sweet Spot by having the ideal range of advertisers (in addition to falling in the Google Trends Market Size Sweet Spot); "HCG diet," despite falling in the Google Trends Sweet Spot, did not fall into the Amazon Market Competition Sweet Spot.

Dr. Yates has gone on to become a leading voice in naturopathic medicine serving women who have PCOS, with a best-selling book, a wildly popular podcast, and recurring appearances on media outlets like NPR, PBS, CNN, ABC, and Fox News. But more than that, she's helped countless women around the world, and it's all because she wasn't deterred by the shadows that the giants in the weight loss market cast. She found a niche and went full steam ahead.

There's another ASK Method client named Chad Collins, whose entrepreneurial journey was conceived because of the competition. In 2012 he went with a colleague to a food court in a mall during their lunch break. From where they were sitting, he could see what appeared to be a LEGO store. He had no clue that LEGO even had its own dedicated stores (didn't people just go to Target to buy a LEGO set?), but seeing the sign above the door with its unmistakable block letters and primary colors made fond childhood memories come flooding back. He insisted they stop in after they finished eating.

In the back of the store was a "Pick-a-Brick" wall where you could fill as many LEGO bricks into a cup as possible and then just pay for the cup. Obviously, the more you could get in, the better. He filled a cup, took it home, and officially introduced his seven-year-old daughter to LEGO. She loved them, and soon began to watch YouTube videos of other kids and families playing with the colorful building blocks.

Her fascination steadily grew, and she asked if they could start their own YouTube channel about LEGO. He said yes, and the second video they ever put up was a tutorial on how to get the most of a single type of brick into one of the cups at the "Pick-a-Brick" wall. The video caught fire within the LEGO enthusiast market and got 50,000 views in a matter of weeks.

As you can appreciate, no logical person would attempt to directly compete with LEGO, not that Chad even had it in his mind to try. But when he heard that there were LEGO events that diehards attended, he thought it would be neat if he and his daughter could go, and maybe put out a video about it on their YouTube channel. Being from Philadelphia, they were in the fifth biggest market in the country, so he thought for sure there had to be an event nearby, but the closest one was several states away. Cue lightbulb moment.

He decided to create an event himself, and that's when Brick Fest Live was born. Nearly 24,000 people attended that very first LEGO event Chad produced. Wondering if the idea was replicable, he found venues in other states, sold tickets, and had similar results, and from there it continued to gain momentum. Fast-forward to today, when Brick Fest Live is the largest touring LEGO event in the United States, attracting tens of thousands of people every weekend a show is held. (As an aside, I'm a certifiable AFOL—that is, an Adult Fan of LEGO—and one of the highlights of my life was delivering the keynote address at the flagship Brick Fest Live event in Philadelphia, attended by over 25,000 LEGO fans, sharing my personal story of how secretly playing LEGO on my bedroom floor as a shy, awkward kid and creating worlds and building things from scratch helped shape me into becoming a successful creator and business builder as an adult. What can I say? I'm a little obsessed with LEGO. :-))

Competition came into play in two main ways here. One, since LEGO is arguably the most valuable toy company in the world, going up against them with a similar product would have been unsmart at best. But, like Dr. Yates, Chad wasn't daunted by their dominance. Since he was an entrepreneur, it merely prompted him to think a little more outside the box and find something he could latch on to within the mega-brand. Two, Chad wasn't in direct competition with other LEGO events; he filled a void for the states that didn't have them. He wasn't trying to reinvent the wheel, but trying to build on what he could see worked. It just so happened that as time went on, his events began to offer things the other events didn't . . . and eventually became the premiere enthusiast event.

My orchid care business wasn't my be-all and end-all passion, but it helped propel me toward building my passion businesses—The ASK Method Company and the software company bucket.io (both of which exist to help entrepreneurs—my favorite people in the world—to better sell and better serve their customers). That's because being dispassionate about a topic can allow you to become passionate about the *process*. And the same thing happened to Chad. Not that he wasn't passionate about LEGO events, but it ultimately served as an entry point.

Today, Chad owns a company called Open World. They produce massive family events that include the original Brick Fest Live (now in dozens of major cities around the nation), as well as Minefaire (an official Minecraft community event that operates under license from Microsoft), Young Innovators Fair (an interactive science event centered around STEM learning), and an upcoming Comic Con for Kids.

There is so much to be learned, gained, and valued from market competition. Whether you're like Sean, who used it as an indicator for which market to pursue, or like Dr. Yates and Chad, who found their perfect niche by knowing where they *couldn't* compete, assessing the competition and letting it push you in the right direction could be the X factor when it comes to your success.

At this point, the Amazon advertising test should have provided clarity around your shortlist of Bullseye Keywords. How many Green lights did it give you? Do you feel confident moving forward, or do you need to take a step back and reassess? My hope is that the past two tests have put you on solid footing and you're ready to head into the last crucial set of tests that are left to apply. They're the final missing pieces you'll need in order to choose your market and verify your business idea. If you're ready, I'm ready.

Market
Must-Haves

You may be wondering how important another series of tests is if your Bullseye Keywords already passed the two Sweet Spot tests with flying colors. Ideal Market Size, check. Optimal amount of Competition, check. You're good to go, right? Not quite yet. There are five Market Must-Haves that are *so* important that if any *one* of the following five traits don't exist within the potential market that you are examining, it needs to be ruled out. Think of the previous tests as the gatekeepers. You made it past the gates—which is huge!—but you still have to make it to the castle.

These five Market Must-Haves are the key attributes that your market must have in order for you to be confident that your potential business idea can truly be profitable. We're going to do a deep dive through each one, and I'll help you refine your top contending business ideas by comparing them against these benchmarks.

If you refer back to Checkpoint 2 on your Choosing Your Green Light Market Worksheet, you'll see that to the right of the Market Competition Sweet Spot traffic lights are the five boxes that indicate each must-have. As we review each of the five traits, you'll check the corresponding box if your business idea fulfills that criterion.

⊛ But there's one thing I need to touch on before we jump in. At the beginning of the book, I mentioned the IN/UP/MAX framework that I commonly teach our clients. For a quick refresh: IN/UP/MAX is a progression-based concept that advises you to launch your business with a low-priced product that acts as a low barrier of entry. It's applicable to and affordable for 100 percent of your customers. That's your IN.

Once your customers are familiar with your business or brand, you can offer a more premium product at a higher price. Because it's more expensive, it's reasonable to assume that not everyone will make the purchase. Typically, you'll find that 10 percent of your customers potentially will. That's your UP.

Finally, you have a top-level offer for customers who are willing and able to spend top dollar on the "bells and whistles" super-premium version of your product or service. The price is roughly 100 times your initial entry product, and you'll find that typically, about 1 percent of your total customer base will complete the purchase. That's your MAX.

As you can see, the IN/UP/MAX approach offers both ascending levels of value for your customers and substantial opportunities for business growth for you. It's a powerful concept and relates to a handful of the Market Must-Haves. So here we go!

Market Must-Have #1: Evergreen Market

The first Market Must-Have is an *evergreen market*. In botany, an evergreen is a plant that has green leaves throughout the year. The same principle applies here. You're looking for a market that continuously self-renews despite season or temperature. And this concept extends beyond the idea of a "stable" market introduced with the Google Trends test. A "stable" market might be stable for *years*. But an "evergreen" market is relevant for *decades*. An evergreen market has longevity and is continually relevant; it's not threatened by external forces like cultural shifts, a temperamental economy, or fleeting interest. The exact opposite definition is that of a fad market.

Contrary to the life cycle of evergreen markets, fad markets have a brief introductory period when the product suddenly hits the market, a growth stage when the product skyrockets into market acceptance, a short maturity stage when the product reaches its market potential, and then a very sharp decline stage when it all but disappears. When we were looking at the Market Size Sweet Spot, we referred to fad markets (like fidget spinners and Hollywood diets) as downward trending markets because, quite literally, the only way they trend is down—and often the decline is sharp and fast.

Go back in time with me to 2011 when Apple released the new iPhone 4s. Let's say you wanted to cash in on its momentum (after all, more than 4 million of them were sold in only the first three days of its being available[1]), so you decided to sell *education and expertise* around iPhone 4s tips. It's a foolproof business move, right? Just imagine all the people looking for a quick and easy tutorial on the hottest new tech gadget on the market! Orders would come flooding in! And they likely would . . . until, inevitably, they wouldn't. The demand would diminish because everyone knows that a new version of the iPhone is right around the corner. Which leaves the present-day version of you with a product that's entirely irrelevant.

To illustrate my point, let's take a look at what Google Trends would show if you entered in "iPhone 4s Tips" circa 2011.

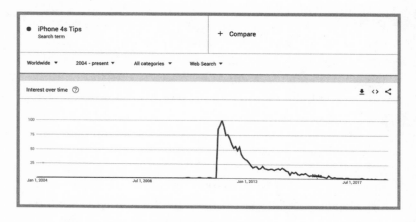

"iPhone 4s tips" 2011 spike and then "spiral of death."

As you can see, prior to September 2011 the line is flat, flat, flat. Then there's a huge spike around the time of the iPhone's release, followed by what I lovingly refer to as the "downward spiral of death." The line's descent is steady and unavoidable. If this were 2011, you could look at that big spike in growth and think you were onto something, but you'd be putting a lot of effort into creating a business model around something that was headed for a downward spiral.

Similar well-known examples of the fad market trap are Beanie Babies, mood rings, Cabbage Patch Kids, hacky sacks, and Pokémon (although they had quite the impressive comeback with Pokémon GO, until that too dropped off). And of course, Scrabble tile jewelry—my own personal cautionary tale about what can happen when you choose a fad market over an evergreen one. I built a successful business around the passing fad, and it proved to be unsustainable in the long term. It was a painful way to learn that a fad market goes up, up, up and then crashes and burns as quickly as it has risen.

The orchid care market is the corollary to that, and I chose it in direct response to my previous experience. I knew I needed to find something that would never go out of style, something that was more than just a sign of the times. So I turned to the oldest, longest-standing hobby in America: gardening. After a little digging (pun intended), I found that an estimated 117 million people (or one in three) per year in the U.S. alone spend time gardening.[2] It was a huge contributing factor to why it made sense to start a business in that space. After passing it through all my tests and finding that "gardening" was too broad, I arrived at the "orchid care" niche.

What happens if we compare "iPhone 4s tips" to "orchid care" in Google Trends? A quick glance proves that an evergreen market will consistently make you money and a fad market won't, because evergreen markets translate to consistent demand and fad markets don't.

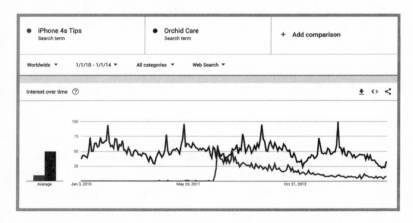

An evergreen market will continue to make you money over time, whereas a fad market only has a short life-span.

Ron Reich nailed it when he chose to enter the potty training puppy market. Caring for dogs, while too enormous to successfully maneuver without paring down and finding a niche, is a perfect example of an evergreen market. Dogs will never go out of style. People will always have them and will always buy products to care for them. The longevity component comes into play not only because of a dog's average life expectancy, but because dog owners tend to always be dog owners; if a furry family member passes away, the owner is likely to get another.

Now take a look at your Bullseye Keywords. Knowing that an evergreen market comes down to longevity, which ideas on your shortlist qualify? Are there any that people will remain interested in over time? For your business ideas that do qualify, proudly put a checkmark in the Evergreen box. Use Google Trends to help you validate. If none of your ideas fulfill that must-have, spend some time brainstorming about how you could adapt your idea to meet the criteria. And if you still hit a dead end, remember that it's okay to go back through the Choose Your Market process as many times as you need to reassess your ideas.

Market Must-Have #2: Enthusiast Market

The second Market Must-Have is called an *enthusiast market*, which describes a market where the buyers are highly enthusiastic about the topic, so much so that they tend to remain buyers for a long period of time. For some, their entire life. Prime examples are antique collectors, sports car lovers, guitar players, home brewers, or orchid enthusiasts. What are you enthusiastic about? How much money have you spent on fostering that interest, and what array of products has that entailed?

While this might seem like a category with an extremely obvious definition, it's important to distinguish the difference between an enthusiast market and a problem/solution market. Enthusiast markets might have immediate problems that need solving—old or damaged guitar strings, for example—but once that problem is solved, the consumer then moves on to other products and areas of interest within that same market. The sky's the limit when it comes to guitar-related purchases, from pick holders to guitar humidifiers (yes, they exist). A problem/solution market is for people who have a problem, their problem gets solved, and they move on with life. Things like a flooded basement or mold removal . . . those are problems no one wants to deal with ever again.

But be aware of the gray area where some markets appear to be problem/solution markets but are actually enthusiast markets. Take something like weight loss. It may seem that once a problem is solved, people move on. Yet people often find themselves in that market for many years, returning time and time again, even though that was never their intention. Not only is there the issue of maintenance (ask anyone who's lost any significant amount of weight, and they'd likely tell you it's a legitimate daily struggle to stay within range), but then there are people who are yo-yo dieters and repeatedly spend money on all different kinds of offerings within the market.

If you're not sure about whether a niche idea falls into an enthusiast market or a problem/solution market, a quick way to find out is to research whether there is a club for the types of people who would buy your product or service. For those who love orchids, there are a ton of orchid societies, online groups, and clubs. For people who brew their own beer, you'll find home brew associations, clubs, or conventions no matter what city you live in. Let me know when you find a mold removal club. (And I don't mean a professional association of mold removers, which I'm sure exists. We're talking about clubs for consumers.)

Early in my entrepreneurial journey when I went looking for evergreen markets, I came up with the idea to launch a business around flea removal with the Bullseye Keyword "kill fleas." Fleas have been a problem forever and they're never going to go away, so I thought my idea was infallible. I could kill it and retire early while fleas continued to infest people's homes and their furry friends. But at that time, I didn't understand the need to avoid the problem/solution market trap, and that's precisely what flea removal is—a problem that requires a solution. Once people solve that problem, that's it; they move on. I neglected to evaluate it from the enthusiast perspective, which is that no one is enthusiastic about fleas. There are definitely no clubs.

Flea removal checked the box for the evergreen market but not the enthusiast market. I did all that work to get a customer without any of the long-term benefits I would have had if I'd put the same effort into acquiring a customer in an enthusiast market. Fleas 1, Ryan 0.

On the other hand, Ron Reich and his potty train puppy market passed both the evergreen and enthusiast tests with ease. At various times, dog owners are interested in purchasing all kinds of dog products—dog toys, dog toilet training, dog obedience, pet insurance, dog food, matching collars and leashes, customized dog tags—and they're usually even enthusiastic about paying the bill. Anything for Fido! (No judgment here, I'm the same way with our dog. In fact, that above list is based on my own past credit card expenses, and I'm slightly embarrassed to admit how much money we've spent on our tiny little four-and-a-half pound friend.)

Ⓑ Let's go back to your Choosing Your Green Light Market Worksheet. Do any of your Bullseye Keywords meet this Market Must-Have? If you're still not sure, go beyond asking yourself whether people will be enthusiastic about the topic—will they be enthusiastic enough about the topic to spend money on it?

And once again, if none of your ideas check this box, feel free to go back to the Brainstorm stage and think through some more viable options. Sometimes you have to go back before you can go forward. It's not failure; it's progress.

Market Must-Have #3: A $10,000 Problem

The third Market Must-Have is what we call a *$10,000 problem.* It's not enough to enter a market that is both evergreen and enthusiast. You need to also focus on solving an *urgent problem in the context of that evergreen and enthusiast market,* and that's where that $10,000 problem comes in. Many people talk about the importance of solving a "$1,000 problem," which is a problem that doesn't necessarily cost $1,000 to solve, but a problem that has a high pain point attached to it (so in other words, a "$1,000 problem"). That's where things start, but it's not where they end.

The *real* question you need to ask yourself is: What is a "$1,000 problem" that under certain circumstances transforms into a $10,000 problem? A problem that has the potential to become 10 times bigger under certain conditions. *That* is what you're looking to solve. And specifically, a $10,000 problem within the context of an evergreen, enthusiast market.

Now, to be clear, I'm not saying the problem you're solving needs to cost $10,000 (or that you need to sell your product for $10,000). That specific figure is just a representative amount to demonstrate that this is a *major* problem; what was once a $1,000 problem has suddenly become a $10,000 problem, and you're looking to not only solve that problem but to know the circumstances around its escalation.

When I teach this in our ASK Academy membership, I find that examples are the best way to articulate the point. Let's use Ron Reich and his decision to choose a niche within the potty train puppy market.

Let's say you're a dog owner and your dog is peeing on the rug. It's a drag, but a common drag. Every puppy does it before it's house-trained (as do many aging dogs when they're declining), so every dog owner deals with the problem. After it happens a few times, it quickly becomes a "$1,000 problem."

But (and this part is important) this $1,000 problem has the potential to become a much bigger, more urgent problem—a $10,000 problem—under the right circumstances.

Let's say you have travel plans in a few weeks and you're set to take the dog with you. Just looking at the calendar and seeing your scheduled flight gives you anxiety. What are you going to do? Every time the dog sees a carpet, he wants to pee. You just know he's going to pee in the airport, he's going to pee on the plane, and you're going to be the crazy dog owner whose dog uses a Boeing 747 as his toilet. The passengers are going to complain, you're going to get kicked off the flight, and you'll be banned from flying any and all commercial aircraft for the rest of your life. What's more, he'll pee in the hotel and you'll have to pay for damages, and ultimately be asked to leave, and your entire trip will be ruined. What was once a $1,000 problem has now suddenly transformed into a $10,000 problem. Both the magnitude of the problem and the urgency to now solve it have suddenly increased tenfold.

Extreme? Yes. But that's what an escalating problem does. It becomes larger than life and requires a radical and immediate solution in order to save a customer's sanity and set the world right again. That particular customer will go to extreme (read: $10,000) lengths to solve it. And this is what you're looking for. A problem where people say, "All right! Enough is enough. I'm going to do something about it, and I'm going to do something about it *now.*"

Say you have a tooth that needs to be removed; that might be a $1,000 problem. It's a nagging problem lingering in the background that you know you need to deal with. But if you wake up one morning with a raging, pounding, unbearable toothache, it quite literally overnight transformed from a $1,000 problem into a $10,000 problem. It's a problem that you will pay any amount of money to solve right away, a problem where you're not going to be shopping around for discounts or the cheapest option. You need help and you need it now. *That* is what you as an entrepreneur are looking for in your market—the $1,000 problem that transforms into a $10,000 problem under certain circumstances.

The good news is that you don't need to figure out your $10,000 problem and corresponding solution right this moment. In choosing your market, you only need to know that the possibility exists and the potential is there. Don't stress out about it right now!

While you relax, here's a less dramatic example. People love orchids. They see one while they're out shopping, buy it, and bring it home. They don't really know how to take care of it, and they've got to figure out how much water to give it, how much humidity it needs, and how and when to fertilize it. It's a problem they'll *eventually* get to solving, when they have time. But then one day, they wake up to find that suddenly the blooms have started to shrivel and drop. In the orchid care market, this is the equivalent of that urgent, $10,000 problem. There's an urgency because consumers don't want their plant to die or lose *all* its blooms, and they know if they're going to save their orchid they need to do something about it *fast*. They don't know if they killed it, if this is just normal, or if they need to do something special to get their orchid to rebloom. But the blooms falling off out of nowhere have created a level of urgency to learn how to properly care for their plant that didn't exist even just a few short days earlier.

Remember the opportunity-based entrepreneur Dana Obleman who created The Sleep Sense Program? Her business is another great example of the $10,000 problem Market Must-Have. If you've got young kids and they're not sleeping through the night, that means you aren't either!

And that's a $1,000 problem you want to solve.

It becomes a $10,000 problem when the night before an important presentation at work, your kids are up all night and you don't get any sleep at all. Hanging above you all night long is the threat of showing up to work the next day looking like you got run over by a truck and being unprepared for the single most important presentation of your week. It's the moment that leads you to say, "Enough is enough!" It just transformed the $1,000 problem lingering in the background into an urgent, *need to solve it now* $10,000 problem that you'll spend virtually any amount of money to fix and resolve.

In these examples, it's not the $1,000 and $10,000 amounts that are important. It's about the multiplication of urgency and importance, and having the foresight to know that the solutions you provide can reach people at the time of their most desperate need. You can find enormous success like Dana or Ron. If you can help an enthusiast solve their urgent $10,000 problem—if someone's toddler starts sleeping through the night, or someone's dog stops peeing where it wasn't supposed to—you can become their trusted advisor for life. You'll be the toddler and/or dog whisperer. They'll tell all their friends. You will have a thriving business in a market that you wisely chose because it gave you the capability to expand.

⊚ If you want a heads-up on the biggest issue with this Must-Have, it's that people try to sell a non-urgent solution. Entry-level solutions (which can also be referred to as the "front end" of your business) need to solve an urgent problem. You could argue the word *urgent* is subjective, but here's my point: If we go back to the IN/UP/MAX model, I had mentioned you want to start with your IN. It's your window into a person's world, your window into a relationship with a new customer. Your IN should be 100 percent focused on solving that $10,000 problem that you've identified in your market.

Ron's IN was not a dog toy; it was a potty training tutorial. His IN product solved an issue that dog owners universally consider urgent: potty training their puppy.

To recap this Market Must-Have, what you're looking for is a $1,000 problem that, under certain circumstances, magnifies into a $10,000 problem. It's a change in circumstances that's led to a change in the level of urgency and intensity of the problem. You're looking for a market where there's a big problem to solve—a $1,000 problem—that has a high likelihood of becoming a much bigger, more urgent problem—a $10,000 problem under the right circumstances.

Ⓑ Head back to your Choosing Your Green Light Market Worksheet and look at your Bullseye Keyword shortlist. Do any of those business ideas solve a $1,000 problem in a person's life that, under certain circumstances, can turn into a $10,000 problem?

If yes, check that box and let's roll to the next on our list. If none of them do, it's back to the drawing board, but now you're armed with more helpful insight than you had last time around.

Market Must-Have #4: Future Problems

The fourth Market Must-Have is having additional *future problems*. What you're looking for here is evidence of additional future problems you can solve for that same customer, above and beyond that first problem you might solve for them. Because once you've taken the time to solve your customer's urgent $10,000 problem up front and set yourself up to become their trusted advisor, you have the opportunity to sell additional products and services down the road. And this comes, most typically, in the form of your UP in the IN/UP/MAX model.

Let me give you a couple of examples of this in action. Take our orchid care business. When someone first reaches out for help, they're typically looking for help solving one of several $10,000 problems, including getting flowers to rebloom on their orchid. Someone who follows the steps we recommend in our *Orchids Made Easy* book and DVD will inevitably get their orchid to rebloom, but will then be faced with a whole other set of challenges, one of which is how to repot their plant. Because, after all, a flourishing orchid will eventually outgrow its pot.

Once you've repotted an orchid for the first time and realized how much of a hassle it is, the appeal of growing orchids without potting material becomes intriguing. So we have an "UP" product in our business called "The Just Add Water Method: How to Ditch the Dirt and Grow Orchids Hydroponically With Nothing but Water." It's an example of solving a future problem that customers didn't yet have when they were first singularly focused on solving their initial, $10,000 problem.

Another example is when someone purchases their first orchid, say a *Phalaenopsis*. But, as they fall deeper and deeper in love with orchids, they may want to add to their collection. So they embark on the journey of bringing home *Cattleyas*, or *Vandas*, or *Oncidiums*, or *Dendrobiums*. Each of these orchids has different needs and growing conditions (a future problem the owner didn't yet have when they brought their first plant home), so we offer an entire series of Orchid Masterclasses for growing and caring for each of the most popular orchid varieties. That first purchase of the book or DVD has set in motion a series of future problems (and potential purchases), as they solve one challenge and move into another along their orchid growing journey. Having customers who come back to you to solve new problems in the future means you need to find fewer new customers (which is expensive) and you make more money from every customer you acquire (which is profitable).

And for the orchid business, there's still more!

Because next there's the topic of chemicals. As one gets deeper into the hobby of orchids, it becomes apparent that there are a number of things you need in order to keep your orchid alive. For someone who wants to go a more organic route, we have a program where we give a number of all-natural alternatives to commercial pesticides and products: Grandma Bea's 47 Garden Home Remedies.

I could go on and on and on, but the point is that in the orchid market, there is evidence of a number of future problems that an orchid enthusiast needs to solve, which lends itself to selling additional products and services to help solve those issues. And that's where your UP comes in.

The same thing happened for Jamal Miller, who, with his wife Natasha, founded The One University (https://theoneuniversity.com), where they help faith-based singles find "the one." What Jamal found in his business was that after he delivered success for his customers, many of them wanted to know the next step: How do they *stay* married and build a long-lasting, thriving partnership? That represented a future problem that customers didn't have when they first arrived at his business. But because he and Natasha became their customers' trusted advisors and earned their loyalty, they were able to continue to serve those customers and solve the next problem (and the next) with future products and services.

For the quintessential scenario, we can look at Ron Reich's business. In the dog market, once the potty training problem is solved, there are endless other issues that customers might face. The dog is a biter. The dog pulls on its leash. The dog barks. The dog runs away. The dog digs up the yard. There are a number of future problems for Ron to solve.

To wrap this up, here's the takeaway: What you want to be looking for is evidence of additional future problems you can solve *in the same market for the same customer*. One where you can solve problem after problem for that same individual, and earn a loyal customer for life.

🕐 It's time to revisit the worksheet to see which of your Bullseye Keywords meet the *Future Problem* criteria. As you look over the niche markets that remain on your shortlist, are there any that provide an immediate problem that you can solve but also have additional problems that will need to be solved in the future for that same customer? After you've vetted your shortlist and/or tested them with any of the above combinations, check the box for *Future Problem* if one or more of your ideas passed the test. If not, try to reimagine or shift your idea so it could comply with this must-have.

Market Must-Have #5: Players with Money

The fifth and final Market Must-Have is *Players With Money*, or PWMs, and this is a phrase I first learned while studying the work of the late, great Gary Halbert, who is widely regarded as one of the greatest direct response copywriters who ever lived. Every market is made up of sub-segments; the challenge is figuring out which of the sub-segments matter. A viable market is one that has

PWMs: people who are willing to spend a large sum of money in one particular area of their lives to address or avoid a recurring problem, or, in many cases, to fuel an important goal, hobby, or personal vision.

The PWM must-have is important on many levels. The first and most glaringly obvious one is that you're selling something that requires your customers to pay money, which clearly means you need to target customers who have money to spend. And second, if you hope to attain any type of substantial business growth, you need to ensure that a percentage of the core audience in your market is willing to invest in the top-dollar super-premium offer you provide, that is, your MAX.

That said, an important detail to keep in mind here is that PWMs don't need to be wealthy in the traditional sense of the word. They just need to show evidence that they're willing to funnel a disproportionate amount of money to a specific area that matters to them.

I've mentioned my venture into the improve memory market several times, but that experience is never more applicable than it is with *this* Market Must-Have. I learned the hard way that the memory improvement space does not include a whole lot of players with money. Our RocketMemory product, while incredibly effective with hundreds of success stories, was ultimately attracting students with limited or no income who wanted to improve their memory for test prep. I think we all know that college students or grad students aren't at the top of the food chain when it comes to spending big bucks. On quantity alone, it earned me good money for a season but ultimately showed me that the best markets must have PWMs to be sustainable.

The orchid care market is actually on the fence here. It's a relatively inexpensive hobby with a small percentage of PWMs. The care of orchids takes some maintenance cost (though not super high), and there's a somewhat limited number of options within the business to offer really high-priced products and services. Fortunately, orchid hobbyists tend to have varying degrees of disposable income, so the additional items our business provided—like the aforementioned DVDs and monthly membership in Green Thumb Club—were feasible and well received by consumers.

If you really want a market where PWMs are prevalent, there are several indisputable ones that come to mind, all of which include big-ticket back-end opportunities that put the MAX in IN/UP/MAX. Therein lies the key nuance: you're looking for evidence of PWMs by finding evidence of MAX offers in the market on which people are already spending money. What do you know for sure that people spend a lot of money on?

A perfect example is golf. People spend *incredible* amounts on the game. Not even taking into account the exorbitant cost that some golf courses charge for a round, there are seemingly endless niche opportunities within the market. The obvious physical products are equipment, accessories, and apparel, but as far as selling *education and expertise* goes, there are dozens of options, including tutorials, lessons, weekly/monthly tips and secrets, and video series.

One of my ASK Method Business Coaching clients, Revolution Golf, focuses on selling *education and expertise* in the golf instruction market. The company was started by a few friends in a bar who shared a love for golf, decided to pursue that passion, and launched their business selling a single golf DVD. They eventually grew to sell dozens of online golf instruction programs, and built a paid membership with tens of thousands of subscribers. Their hard work paid off in a big way, because a few short years later, Revolution Golf was acquired by NBC for an undisclosed sum, with a payday worth tens of millions of dollars.[3]

The revenue potential of golfers continues to rise with regular expenditures on high-end golf vacations at world-class resorts or expensive tickets to premier golf tournaments like the PGA Championship or British Open. If you wanted to entertain a MAX offering in that market, it could include something like a U.S. Masters experience where you take groups on trips and they get to rub shoulders with the players or attend special VIP dinners.

The lesson here is that when looking at niche markets that center around hobbies, the more money that's required to invest in that hobby, the more likely you'll have the presence of PWMs. Golf is clearly up there. Another good example is the yacht market. Owning or chartering a yacht is a very expensive hobby and will naturally attract PWMs. Alternatively, chess is a low-cost hobby. What do you need to play a game of chess? A board and pieces. It's something anyone can do for free in the park. While you can certainly offer a board made with premium materials like marble or crystal or a rare hand-carved wood, there's only so much a chess customer would pay for a high-end game. And even if someone would pay, say, $1,000, for a premium chess board, they'll likely do that only once, as a gift to themselves or someone else.

You ideally want to choose a market where PWMs occupy as much of the market as possible because it provides an optimal number of people who are able to purchase higher-priced products and services from you. Think about the dog market example. There are a ton of dog owners who are PWMs, and they'll go to extreme lengths and spend inordinate amounts of money in the name of caring for their dog.

As extensive and/or outlandish as some dog products or services may sound, they all exist because there's a demand—from things like organic food and high-end grooming to fancy dog spas and lavish doggy hotels. There's a "chateau" in Florida that provides dogs with their own suites, complete with a king-size sleigh bed, a flat-screen television, a personal overnight attendant, an on-site gourmet chef, a day spa that features blueberry facials, and a Zen wellness center to "soothe the soul and replenish the body."[4] In Munich, there are "dog lodges" that offer expertly trained dog-sitters who provide grooming and exercise regimes and physiotherapy and wellness treatments, which include a 90-minute therapy session followed by orthopedic and neurological analysis.[5]

Maybe to get there, the dogs can fly on a jet chartered specifically for them and their owners. Japan Airlines now offers a dog-friendly service,[6] where for the mere price of 150,000 yen, people can fly with their dog on a pet-friendly plane (fear not, several veterinarians are on board), stay in a dog-friendly hotel, and go sightseeing with provided transportation during a three-day canine holiday.

Ron Reich didn't just choose a market where he knew a lot of people would buy a $100 short online course on potty training their puppy. It was also a market where he knew that some of those *same* people could buy big-ticket items, whether it was special flight accommodations, diamond dog collars, or gold-plated water bowls (none of which Ron sells, but you get my point).

Notice that I used the word "would" when describing the $100 online course, but "could" when referencing the expensive accessories. Not that people with a limited income wouldn't splurge or invest in a multi-thousand-dollar item, but choosing a market with people who are known to commonly do it is an essential facet of the PWM Market Must-Have.

Before we move on, I want to repeat the most fundamental piece of information I've covered in regard to choosing a market that has PWMs. It's extremely important to me that if nothing else, you walk away with this understanding: look for evidence of PWMs by finding evidence of MAX offers that are already being purchased in the market.

How? Head back to Google and start searching for examples of your Bullseye Keywords along with the addition of a big-ticket item. Try buzzwords like "retreat," "certification," "mastermind," "mentoring," "tour," or "trip" for starters. For example, if you typed in "home brewing retreat" you'd see a few results come up. That's a great sign there's interest! If you tried "home brewing workshop," you'd again see several results. You'd also see that some of those workshops cost a couple thousand dollars to attend. Another great sign! This simple Google test helps shed light on the market demand and helps you gauge purchase plausibility. Because, ultimately, the last thing you want to do is choose a market where you face a ton of resistance to spending money and therefore limit your profit potential.

⊛ Time to go back to Checkpoint 2 in your Choosing Your Green Light Market Worksheet. To determine whether or not your business niche ideas align with the fifth Market Must-Have, ask yourself this: *Are there players with money in your potential market to whom you can sell big-ticket items?* It's not a question to determine what those items or opportunities are, only that they could feasibly exist.

With that, I'd like to touch one last time on how the IN/UP/MAX model applies to all of this. The *$10,000 Problem* maps back to your IN. It's all about solving an urgent problem in the context of an enthusiast market. Your UP is all about solving a *Future Problem* for the same customer in the same market. And finally, *Players With Money* is where your MAX comes in. You want to make sure you verify there are players with money in your market who are spending big bucks, and then in time have a corresponding MAX offer to serve them.

By now, all your Bullseye Keywords have been run through all five of the Market Must-Haves. You've compared your niche market ideas against criteria that set your potential business up for success. How's your list looking? Do any of your ideas have each box checked?

It's important to note that if all five areas don't have a checkmark, it doesn't mean your idea is a bad idea that needs to be disregarded completely. But it does mean you'll want to look at the particular must-have it's missing, and think about how you could position things differently so that it does fulfill each necessary criterion.

You might have to do some research, think more creatively about your idea, or perhaps get some inspiration from other industries. If you still can't see a way to satisfy all five crucial elements of a successful market, you'll want to go back to either the Market Size or Market Competition steps and come up with alternative ideas that are still in your Sweet Spot areas but that do fulfill all five Market Must-Haves. If you still can't get a winning idea that checks each box, then head back to the Brainstorm stage and start the process again.

Please remember this is an iterative process! Don't get discouraged by having to go backward in order to step further forward. The truth is that many people have to go back through parts of the Choose Method multiple times (and sometimes more times than they'd like to admit). And it's no different when I go through the process myself.

Remember that this is your single most important decision as an entrepreneur: Who are you going to serve? What market are you going to enter? It's worth spending time here. In the end, your future business will be all the better for it because you took the time to scrutinize your ideas from every angle and eliminate the ones that won't lead to a viable market choice. Be committed to the tightest, strongest business idea possible. If you do this, you're setting yourself up to be that much more likely to succeed.

The next section is where it all comes together. When you're ready to move to the final stage, let's begin consolidating your results and moving forward with a front-running idea. Are you ready to Choose?

Progress Summary

You've just completed Stage 2 in the Choose Method Process!

Here's a quick summary of your progress so far.

Stage 1—BRAINSTORM

☑ Step 1—Model Brainstorm

☑ Step 2—Market Brainstorm

☑ Step 3—Business Idea Brainstorm

STAGE 2—TEST

☑ Step 4—Bullseye Keyword

☑ Step 5—Market Size Sweet Spot

☑ Step 6—Market Competition Sweet Spot

☑ Step 7—Market Must-Haves

STAGE 3—CHOOSE

☐ Step 8—Choose Your Market

☐ Step 9—The Final Step to Launch

STAGE 3

CHOOSE

Screw it, just do it!

The end is . . . or rather, the beginning, is near. This is the last section of the book but the start of what will surely be an exciting entrepreneurial journey. You've followed the Choose Method all the way to this point, which means you've put in the time, effort, research, patience, imagination, and diligence to vet your ideas and identify an ideal market that holds the promise of success.

So here you are. It's time to jump into the water, which hopefully doesn't feel as perilous as it once did. If you're still feeling a bit queasy, remind yourself that the scariest moment is always right before you start—that split second before you hurl yourself out of the plane, walk out on the stage, or sign your name on the dotted line.

You've done so much groundwork to get to where you are, and it's led you to this critical juncture. Now you want to grab your Choosing Your Green Light Market Worksheet. As you went through each Market Must-Have, you should have put a checkmark in the appropriate box on the worksheet as you found evidence of that individual trait for each particular keyword. If that's complete, it's time to determine whether each key-word is a Red, Yellow, or Green light.

For any Bullseye Keyword that has three or fewer Market Must-Haves, the idea gets a Red light. If an idea has four of the Market Must-Haves, it gets a Yellow light. And if one or more of your ideas has all five of the Market Must-Haves, it gets a Green light.

Now to officially bring it all together, take the Bullseye Keywords that got a Yellow or Green light on both of the Checkpoint 2 tests—that is, on the Market Competition Sweet Spot test *and* the Five Market Must-Haves test. Add them to the shortlist of Bullseye Keywords in Checkpoint 3 at the bottom of your worksheet, which is where you'll apply the final Red light, Yellow light, or Green light, here in this final Choose Stage.

How do you assign your final Red, Yellow or Green light in Checkpoint 3? The lowest value of either of the Checkpoint 2 tests (Market Competition Sweet Spot and the Five Market Must-Haves) determines your overall market test result. So, for example, if one of your keywords has a Green test result for Market Competition Sweet Spot and a Yellow test result for the Five Market Must-Haves, your overall market test result for that keyword will be Yellow, because that's the lowest of the two results.

ⓑ Go ahead and calculate your results in Checkpoint 3 now.

How's it looking?

You now have your final shortlist of Bullseye Keywords, and you are officially on the threshold of choosing your market.

And it's at this point that you may be feeling an array of emotions. Everything from *I've got this and I know **exactly** which one I'm going to choose* through to *I'm torn between two ideas* and *I'm not sure if **any** of these ideas are* *ones I want to pursue!* Or perhaps you are feeling like you know which option to take, and you've known it for the longest time, but doing it scares you out of your mind. Or you may even feel a combination of all of the above!

And that's normal. This is a big moment you are standing on the edge of. You've gone through multiple tests, come up with possibly dozens of business ideas and keywords, and likely looped back around a number of times as various ideas hit Red lights. You've summoned your strength over and over and it's all led you to this moment, right here, right now.

In the next few pages you will choose your market.

But in the time I still have you before you do that, there are some things I'd like to share, things that I wish someone had shared with me when I first embarked on my entrepreneurial journey over a decade ago and was on the verge of choosing my market. Sometimes you just need someone to shoot it to you straight, you know?

Choose Your Market

I want to have a completely open, honest, and raw conversation with you about this decision you're making. Let's start by just acknowledging that choosing your market isn't like choosing what froyo flavor you want in your cup. This decision creates many more ripples in your life, and knowing that tends to drum up some profound emotions at both ends of the spectrum. In the entrepreneurial world, we don't like to talk about this much because it feels like inviting or admitting weakness, but the reality is that entrepreneurship is emotional. I don't want to be one who downplays your emotions as you come to this big decision.

On one hand, you're probably filled with a lot of hope. The potential of what lies ahead could have game-changing repercussions, whether that's in regard to financial freedom, the freedom of being your own boss, the chance to share an idea with the world, or all of the above. At long last, you made it through the Choose Your Market process, but that's nothing compared to how long you've likely been dreaming about what this next phase of your life could look like.

On the other hand, you might be scared out of your mind. We're all afraid for varying reasons. And some of those reasons are entirely reasonable. We don't want to lose all our money. We don't want to wreck our marriage or our kids' lives or our own self-confidence. We don't want to lose what we already have that's good. In other words, there's risk. No doubt about it.

A life lesson I've learned over the years is that often, the thing that you're most afraid of doing is the thing you need to do the most. My parents didn't go to college. They're the first people in each of their families to graduate high school, and there wasn't a whole lot that they could teach me about business and excelling in college and beyond. But there's one thing that they taught me that's always stuck with me. My parents used to say, "Ryan, there are only two things you need in this life: courage and grit."

I've followed that advice throughout my life. In fact, in some cases, *clung* to that advice might be more accurate. I remember my very first day at Brown as an incoming freshman. I met all of these other students who had just come from the best prep schools in the country. The guy in the dorm across the hall from me had literal French maids moving him in. All I could think was, *What am I doing here? How am I going to survive in this world?*

I went to a public high school in a working-class neighborhood where getting into an Ivy League school happened to a student once in a blue moon. Growing up, I'd always held multiple jobs and the closest I had ever come to a French maid was watching the movie *Clue*. I was so overwhelmed and afraid for my first day of classes that I didn't sleep at all the night before; I just cried in my pillow all night long.

Entrepreneurial success is not about not being unafraid. You are about to make a decision that naturally evokes a lot of fear and trepidation. I'll tell you what I tell my two sons, Henry and Bradley: Courage is about taking action in spite of that fear. That's what courage is all about.

Of course, I say that now. Back then, I was practically paralyzed by my own insecurity. I thought courage meant waiting until the lights went out before I cried. Succumbing to my fear and crawling into a hole every time failure was an option would have felt like a peaceful refuge. But that's where the second part of my parents' advice around grit comes into play. Grit means you keep crawling out of the hole.

The summer before I started high school, I got accepted into the Summer Youth Music School, or SYMS, a regional music program for "gifted" musicians. It was an incredible opportunity, and I thought I was the coolest person alive. I packed my bags for what was surely going to be the most amazing summer of my life, but right after I got there, I realized I was the most *un*talented kid in the entire program. I'm being completely serious. I called my parents repeatedly, telling them, "Pick me up. I can't do it. I wanna go home." But those character-building parents of mine wouldn't hear of it.

There was a concert for all the parents at the end of the summer where, in addition to all the students playing in a giant orchestra together, we each had to do a solo performance. Because I played two instruments, piano and saxophone, I had to do two solos. I was not only the worst pianist in the entire program, but also the worst saxophonist. And I had to get up there and play on a stage, by myself, while having a panic attack (more or less) and plagued with high levels of terror and humiliation. Twice.

I wish I could tell you that the story has a happy ending, but I'd be lying. I royally botched both solos and hardly got through either of them. The look of pity from my instructors and fellow students was unmistakable, and I took what was left of my pride and counted the moments until the concert ended so I could finally go home.

I ran toward my parents afterward, and my mom said, "We're so proud of you! How do you feel?"

I looked at her like she had three heads.

"Horrible," I said. "I feel horrible."

To that my dad said, "Then just imagine how much worse you'd feel had you quit."

Those words stuck with me for a long time.

Years later, when I was 18 years old and the captain of my high school soccer team, I was invited to try out for a premier league team that focused on Olympic development. I had played years of competitive soccer at that point, so I jumped at the opportunity and made it past three rounds of cuts to squeak onto the team. The first game we played, I sat the bench the entire game. It was the very first time in my life that had happened. I thought it was a fluke, some weird one-time thing where the coach overlooked me, until it happened again at the second game and then the third.

For the next 15 games, I never got off the bench. The coach didn't give me even one minute of playing time in one single game. It was similar to how I felt at SYMS when I'd gone from a big fish in a small pond to a tiny fish in a huge sea; I went from the best at one level to the absolute worst in the next.

I understand what it feels like to get really excited about launching into something new and then not having it work out. I know how devastating it can be when you take a chance and then end up falling flat on your face. But don't quit. Don't let this endeavor be something you start only to let the fear of what failure might mean allow you to run out of the side exit (or the dorm room, or the stage, or the field).

Out of all the questions I get from people who are at the same point where you are right now in this process, the majority of them revolve around *fear* and *failure*. What happens if it all suddenly goes south? Or worse yet, never gets off the ground? Should they keep their day jobs? Are they going to be successful right away? Can I tell them for certain? As much as I want to curb their anxiety, I'm forced to tell them that the only certainty in being an entrepreneur is living with uncertainty. It's an unavoidable truth that not enough entrepreneurs publicize.

Working a job with a specific wage where you receive a paycheck every single month, that's certainty. Job security through tenure, accrued vacation days, and matching 401(k) contributions, that's certainty. Clocking out and not taking your work home with you at night, that's certainty. If you're looking for certainty, I wish I could tell you with 100 percent confidence that you won't fail, but the truth is, you might.

The good news is that, from a market standpoint, you've mitigated the risk as much as you possibly can. You've vetted the possible markets and found one or more that check all the boxes for success. However, making that choice now and building your business from here is still a bet. *But* it's a different kind of bet than just throwing your time and hard-earned money into the latest fad market. The kind of bet you're making now is betting on yourself. And I'll tell you now what I wish someone had told me when I was where you are right now, and what I learned to appreciate from my friend Stu McLaren: *There is no better bet than betting on yourself.* So whatever market you choose, most importantly, choose *you.*

I find myself toeing the line between a pep talk and a disclaimer whenever I talk to entrepreneurs about uncertainty and failure. I want to prepare them for the worst but give them reason to hope for the best. The truth is that I'm uncomfortable with the level of uncertainty that this line of work provides. In fact, I would even go so far as to say that I'm a risk-averse entrepreneur. If it's surprising to hear me say that, I get it. From where you sit, I've gambled and won more than I've lost. But that doesn't mean I haven't spent years trying to overcome the daily threat that my profession hangs over my head.

When people come to me for coaching or take my courses and hear me speak confidently about how to avoid the common traps of starting a business, what they might not put together is that I'm doing all of this *because* I'm scared of the uncertainty. And there are some days when I'm scared to death. I developed these strategies as a way to help myself mitigate risk as best I could. For me, the antidote to a lifelong fear of not measuring up has been a constant quest of achieving *mastery.* Or, in this case, *mastering*—and in that process *demystifying*—the secret to launching a new business with near 100 percent success. Once I figured out that I was onto something, I wasted no time in testing the methods over and over again and then sharing them with entrepreneurs and aspiring entrepreneurs who were similarly ambitious and driven, but also sometimes held back by that same fear of failure.

My urge to reduce risk is innate. When I was growing up, I went the extra mile on everything I did because I thought it would somehow guarantee that I wouldn't come up short. And I couldn't turn off the insatiable motivation to excel and eliminate any chance to the contrary.

We did not have a lot of money growing up. We rarely went out to eat and we didn't go on expensive vacations. We never did a lot of stuff that other kids did. Money was tight and there was always talk about not having enough to be able to afford this or that. My parents were really matter-of-fact when they talked about it, though. They didn't purposefully transfer monetary stress onto me; they were just trying to explain where we stood and set proper expectations around the kind of life we were going to live.

But transfer it did. I became an overcompensating workhorse. This was both in response to money (I didn't want to stress them out—I wanted to contribute) and because my parents set such an incredibly strong example with their own work ethic. My dad worked nights, and my mom was a hairdresser who had a salon in the basement of our house. She was an early riser so she'd wake up to welcome my dad home and then start taking clients at 5:00 A.M. (mainly older female teachers who wanted their hair teased out before school). She made sure my sister and I were awake right along with her because we had all our chores to get done.

We grew up in New Hampshire, and the winters were rough. Before the sun came up, my parents would have us out there with them shoveling snow—the driveway, the porch, even the roof, because it tended to cave in under the weight of the ice. If we weren't shoveling snow, we were raking leaves, stacking firewood, weeding the gardens and flowerbeds, or mowing the lawn. If we were indoors, we were dusting, vacuuming, cleaning the windows, or doing the dishes.

And that was just the school-year schedule. Summer was far more intense. From May through August, the rule was my sister and I had to do four hours of work and one hour of reading every day before we could play. We woke up, consulted the list, put in our four hours, read a book, and then went on with our day.

I wasn't resentful of it in the least. I thrived on filling my time, as if the more I did, the more valuable I was. In fact, could I do more? How much more?

In middle school I became obsessed with the spelling bee. When I beat every other fourth grader in my class, it was off to the races.

The next phase had me competing against the whole school, and after beating all the 5th-, 6th-, 7th-, and 8th-graders, I was to represent the school at the state championship, at nine years old competing against teenagers. I studied so hard. There was a booklet with all the words in it, and every night my dad would run spelling drills with me for hours at a time. It was never enough. After my parents tucked me into bed and said good night, I sat under the covers with a flashlight to review the booklet until my eyelids refused to stay open.

When the day finally arrived and I took my place on stage at the state championship, I choked. I messed up on the word *sandal* in the third round. It still haunts me to this day. I successfully spelled words like *perspicacity* and *cerulean*. But I messed up on *sandal*. Sandal is such an easy word.

In high school, I did nearly everything—soccer, band, track, drama, serving as student representative for the school board, and treasurer of my class. I would be at school early in the morning, and by the time I finished soccer or track or drama or jazz band, I'd get home well past dark, eat a late dinner, and then stay up until the middle of the night doing homework for all my Advanced Placement classes until my dad was either waking up or getting home from his night shift.

In the later part of high school, I applied for early action to Brown. Some colleges offer it, Brown obviously being one of them, and it's where you apply early in order to hear an early acceptance decision. Once again, mitigating risk. When everyone else at my high school was finding out their fate in April, I had known mine since November the prior year. Of course, the real reason I applied early was that I couldn't bring myself to send in my Harvard application. It was filled out and ready, but I was horrified at the prospect of not making the cut. So I did early action with Brown because if I got in there, that meant I didn't have to apply to Harvard after all. When Brown accepted me, I had nothing to lose because I was in. Harvard would never get the chance to reject me.

I've spent years of my life mastering a tightly choreographed dance between taking the risk of putting in hard work, knowing I could still not measure up, and using my work ethic to resource my way to mitigating as much risk as possible. Eventually (and thankfully) I learned how to risk well, developing the essence of what would become the Choose Your Market framework.

Going through the Choose Method myself—long before it had a name or could be considered a teachable methodology—was my own personal version of putting all my chips into the pot. It was very measured, and I only moved forward once I had data validation and a Green Light.

If you've been immersed in the business world or entrepreneurship space for any amount of time, you've probably seen that most people who have jumped into the seven-, eight-, and nine-figure range experienced the ramen noodle–eating season of their lives, or for some, way more than a season—Oprah Winfrey, John

Paul DeJoria (Paul Mitchell), Larry Ellison (Oracle), and Howard Schultz (Starbucks), just to name a few.

Does it feel disheartening for those who haven't struggled, as if in order to have a good life they first have to tank? As helpful as going through periods like that can be—at the very least, desperation can be a powerful lesson in humility and provide a baseline to always refer back to when you need some motivation—is it really necessary? In order to go from good to great, do you have to go to *ramen*?

A mentor told me, in the midst of one of my sinking ships (read: impending business failure, cue panic), that everything would seem less catastrophic if I just reframed my perspective. It was a pretty obvious statement, but I asked her to decode it for me anyway.

She said, "It's all in how you think about it. What if instead of it being between winning or losing, there was only winning or *learning*? Then no outcome would be considered failure."

It changed my perspective forever.

Just think: if you reframe everything as an experiment, then the whole point could be about testing, analyzing, and improving. If something didn't work out, you could just pivot and experiment with a different variable. It could be all about learning, even if the only thing you learn in some cases is humility.

To be clear, I'm not insinuating that you be flippant about your business ventures, nor am I trying to minimize the hazards involved in launching a business. For all I know, you're about to put all your eggs in one basket and what you stand to lose could feel like (or actually be) everything and more. I'm only saying that if you reframe your perspective about it, the weight of the world might not feel as heavy.

You win, or you learn.

When I embraced that thought process, it immediately relieved me from the pressure of having to get it right. By giving myself the permission to fall short, I didn't have to write myself off as an epic failure if I did indeed fall. By giving myself that grace, I was more apt to keep crawling out of the hole. Courage and grit, I tell you.

If we focus on mastering the process, we detach ourselves from the outcome. The truth is, as it pertains to business, we have very little control over whether people pay money in exchange for our products or services. We can *influence* it, but we can't control it. And perhaps counterintuitively, I've learned that when I detach myself from the outcome and focus on the process, that's when results actually come. It's all fine and good to have big goals and big visions for your business; I certainly have them for mine. But I've learned the secret is to put it all out there and then forget about it to a certain degree. You can't spend all your energy worrying about whether or not you'll be successful. Instead, just focus on each step as it comes; focus on the process.

We all know that a journey of a thousand miles begins with a single step. In the world of business, that first step is choosing your market. You've gone above and beyond in your effort to get that right; you clearly want your journey to start off on solid footing. The rest of the trek becomes a mix of ups, downs, inclines, declines, and flat periods of seemingly little progress. Your perspective during each of those instances will be a determining factor in how readily you move forward. In the end, you will need to remind yourself *why* you're taking these steps in the first place. When your *why* becomes strong enough, you can endure almost any *how*, no matter how difficult the path ahead may seem.

From the public's perspective, Kristi Kennedy started Bee Friendly in response to bullying. During her original soft launch of the business, bullying was well on its way to being a serious national public health issue, so her business was a warranted response to an escalating need. But you and I know that the steps she took to create an effective program were because of her son. Due to his falling victim to bullies, Kristi had skin in the game.

But it went even deeper than that. Kristi knew that the kids bullying her son could be the victims of bullying themselves; she knew that it was a perpetual cycle that often started with learned behavior.

How did she know?

Her son being bullied at school occurred around the same time she discovered that her estranged husband had been severely bullied in his youth. While it certainly didn't condone his behavior, it explained it a bit more. She therefore realized the long-term repercussions of what being bullied could do to someone, and what it could mean for them as they grew into adults.

It got so bad that after her husband left, Kristi ultimately made the painful decision to become what's been referred to as a "widow of circumstance." She traded in a "comfortable" life to start over with nothing in order to protect her children.

She had to do what she could to intervene. It went beyond her son, herself, and her other kids. She had to step in on behalf of every child who might allow others' unkindness to dictate who they become.

The *why* for starting your business certainly doesn't have to resemble heroism. The point is that pining for success does not a successful entrepreneur make. What's underneath that desire?

Sure, when Charlie Wallace launched Guitar Mastery Method, he needed money. His *why* could have very well been wrapped up in wanting to live out his visions of grandeur as a rock star and become rich. But the truth was that every time Charlie played guitar with his band, he felt alive. He couldn't imagine not having that outlet, and it boggled his mind to think that millions of people out there weren't fostering their own love of music.

The thought of being able to help others tap into their passion was life giving for Charlie, but there was also another driving force behind choosing his market and launching his business. Charlie's father, who had been an incredibly hard-working man all his life, suffered a stroke while sitting next to Charlie in an airplane on an international flight. He was hospitalized, nearly lost mobility in half his body, and then endured months of rehab. During those months, instead of being able to focus on getting better, his dad was too busy worrying about when he could get back to work because money was so tight.

That was around the time Charlie launched his business, and after months of hard work, he grew his business to the point where he got to pick up the phone, call his dad, and tell him, "Dad, you can quit your job and never work another day in your life. You don't have to worry about money anymore. It's my turn to take care of you now."

Charlie's *why* was twofold: follow his dream *and* take care of the people he loves. The fact that his business resulted in him having financial success, a respected brand, and making *Entrepreneur* magazine's list of the Top 10 Entrepreneurs under 30 was an incredibly convenient side effect of his primary intentions.

Remember Robert Torres? His stint in real estate marketing is what ultimately set him on the path to launching

The People and Properties Academy. If you recall way back in Step 3, Robert's "I want to" statement was "I want to help *real estate agents convert leads*." One could reasonably look at that and assume they know his *why*, but they couldn't be more wrong.

Robert was born in Guadalajara, Jalisco, Mexico. And when he was a young boy, his mom was insistent that moving to America would be the catalyst to provide Robert with a better life, which she vowed to make happen. When red tape around securing a visa threatened to cancel their plans, Robert and his mom entered the country incognito and under the radar.

This, of course, would have implications, none of which Robert saw coming. In fact, Robert had no idea he had entered the country illegally at all until after the September 11 attacks when he decided to join the Marines and the recruiter asked him for his social security number. Not knowing it, he called his mom to ask. That's when he found out he didn't have a social security number, due to the fact that he wasn't born in the U.S., and therefore couldn't join the military. That's also when he found out not being able to join the military was the least of his worries.

Of all the problems his lack of paper trail posed, the immediate one was that it made him unemployable; no one would hire him without proper documentation to prove who he was. That's when he set his eyes on becoming an entrepreneur. If other people couldn't give him a job, he would create his own. He knew what a hard worker he was, and he knew he was capable of building something worthwhile. Because of the DREAM Act legislation, Robert started the process of becoming a permanent resident. He chose a market, launched two different businesses, and now provides for his wife and daughters the life that he didn't get to have.

What are you after? What is your *why*? Is the journey you're embarking on about attaining more money or acclaim or friends? Or is it about attaining more life? Is it about gaining freedom, making an impact, and leaving your legacy?

When I was 30 years old, I was given a gift. Shortly after my first son, Henry, was born, I started unexpectedly losing weight and began feeling tired all the time. I chalked it up to the sleepless nights of being a new dad while at the same time trying to run my company. Tylene asked me to apply for life insurance in case something were to ever happen to me, and when I got the results back from my application, I found I was denied coverage on the grounds of blood test results that came back off the charts. The next day, I went in to see a doctor and was promptly rushed to the emergency room and told I should have been in a coma. They couldn't believe I was conscious and functioning.

I quickly learned that my kidneys were shutting down, my liver was failing, and my pancreas had stopped working. It turned out I was an undiagnosed Type I juvenile diabetic, and I had slipped into a state known as diabetic ketoacidosis—and I was dying. I spent the next 10 days in the intensive care unit clinging to life. I emerged from that experience realizing that none of us is promised tomorrow. Nothing gives you clarity of purpose like coming to terms with your own mortality. And today, when I think about my life, I think about my two boys, Henry and Bradley, and how grateful I am for the opportunity to be their dad. For me that's what life is all about.

That time in the hospital also served as the catalyst to create the ASK Method (and eventually the Choose

Method) and to focus my life toward teaching other entrepreneurs to do what I had done: how to launch and grow a successful business—and how to mitigate risk as much as possible at every single step along the way.

Around that same time came the shift in my perspective: the reframing of "you win or you learn" instead of the customary win-or-lose mindset. The culmination of those two things fundamentally changed my path.

Having joy in entrepreneurship—that is, in the act of being an entrepreneur—is actually the goal. How many days can you string together and really enjoy them? In my opinion, to do that means never setting an arrival point. It's about the feeling of moving in the car as opposed to reaching the destination. It's the anticipation of it and being in the constant state of momentum.

Set the outcome, know what you want to do, and then just focus on the process. There's transformation in terms of what you're delivering to your market, but there's also the transformation you're delivering for yourself in this process; that is, what you're looking to personally achieve within yourself.

You've gone through the entire process of choosing your market, and now you have a business idea that has the potential to be whatever you want it to be.

You have arrived at an important moment in this book . . . and in your life.

The time to choose.

You have all the information you need. You are ready. You know there are only two outcomes from here: you either win or you learn . . . and both of those are really a win. Now there's just one thing left to do.

Choose.

🐝 What do you want your business to be? *Why?* What are you after? What are you going to do when you get there? The only thing you need to do now is simply complete the final section (Checkpoint 3) in the Choosing Your Green Light Market Worksheet.

Perhaps there is only one Green light market at your final checkpoint . . . or perhaps you get to choose from a few. Either way, this is your moment to confidently decide which direction you are going to take.

Once you've made your choice, I highly recommend you grab the biggest, thickest marker you can find so you can draw a bold, giant circle around it on your worksheet.

This is *your* business idea, and once you've chosen it, you can finally get to work.

To paraphrase what one of my mentors once taught me, "The best time to get started was 25 years ago . . . But the second best time is *today.*"

In other words, there might never be a perfect moment. But there's no better time to *choose* than right here, right now.

I have no doubt you'll give it all you have. As you make this decision and take the first step toward building your business, I've tried to create a clear path so you don't have to cut through all the weeds and thorn bushes like I had to. I've tried to alleviate as much margin of error, to help you be as successful as possible out of the gate. And now the rest is up to you. My hope is that you take the countless stories that you've just heard and use them as motivation to go from good to great; use them as inspiration to live with courage and grit; or use them as a manual for what not to do. Whichever is applicable.

Just promise me that your process won't end with this book.

Because for *you*, and *your* story? This is just the beginning.

The Final Step to Launch

Ask

You're in the best position you could possibly be right now. You've chosen a well-vetted niche market, you have a solid business model, and you may even know the general vicinity of what your products or services could be. You have a baseline of essential information that many (dare I say most) budding entrepreneurs don't have, and you're well on your way to having what you need in order to launch a successful business.

When I coach entrepreneurs, I use the concept of concentric circles to illustrate the gradation of the Choose Your Market process. What I find the coolest about concentric circles, and why I feel they're applicable to this entire process, is that no matter how many you have, they're all the same distance apart; they're in perfect proportion to each other. Their congruent radius and circumference means that each layer of the circle is equally substantial.

For the purposes of this book and to align with the subject matter at hand, this concentric circle illustration consists of just three circles. You'll probably be happy to hear that we've already covered the outer two, which means the only thing left to address is the innermost one.

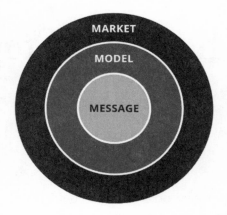

Imagine the outside circle is "Market." It represents the first and biggest decision an entrepreneur makes because its construction holds all the inner layers of the circle together. You've learned everything there is to learn about this Market circle—from the various types, to the traps to avoid, to the proof of its vast importance—and then you brainstormed, tested, and chose your niche.

If you head inward, the next circle would be "Model." We've been working under the assumption that the recommended model of selling *education and expertise* was your focus, but as you'll recall, there are different choices out there. The content of the Model circle also includes elements like the Product Grid, the IN/UP/MAX Framework, and how IN/UP/MAX fits with the five Market Must-Haves. All work together to form an incredibly tight-fitting infrastructure geared toward success.

The next concentric circle is the third and final: your "Message" is your innermost core layer. Now that you've *chosen* your market, what are you going to *say* to your market? How do you reach them in the first place? How do you make sure you connect with them at a deep emotional level? How do you make sure you address their *true* needs, wants, and desires? Is there a way to enter the conversation already going on inside your market's mind? A way to know exactly what they want? Not what they *think* they want, but what they *really* want, and more specifically what they really want to *buy*?

I told you before that my main concern is making sure you feel equipped to move forward from here. You certainly have enough fuel to get you going, yet in order for you to have the most comprehensive and preparatory view of what lies on the other side of this book, I feel obligated to prep you for this critical core work that's rapidly approaching.

Remember back in the first chapter when I talked about how *Choose* was essentially a prequel to my first book? How despite hearing about all the wins of my readers after they read *Ask*, some still struggled because they chose a bad market? No matter how prepared they were after implementing the ASK Method, doing so in the wrong market was met with unavoidable failure. I realized I had to write *this* book to explain how I chose my successful markets in the first place and how to follow that same process. Using that same rationale, I then realized I had to include *this final chapter* to explain the importance of what comes immediately after choosing. In the case of the circles, what lives in the center: your Message.

If geometry's not your thing, we can revisit our trusty boat example. You've finally surveyed all the bodies of water, looked at all the possibilities, and chosen a certain river with a proven current. Its depth, width, and flow rate are ideal for your boat. You're on the dock with oars in hand and prepared to shove off, but that's when it hits you: *Is this even the right type of boat?* You just spent so much time investigating every aspect of your potential river, you didn't even think about whether or not you had the right vehicle to navigate the waters well. So in the interest of time (and brain space), you quickly assume that any ol' boat is fine; you just need one that looks sturdy enough to successfully get you downriver.

Could that work out in your favor? Possibly . . . but how long are you planning to ride? Are you picking others up on the way? What kinds of obstacles will you be navigating around? These are the questions any experienced waterperson would ask, because they know all too well that the intended use of the boat is what dictates its hull shape, length, and construction material. To give you the best shot at a successful ride, you need to have a clear sense of its purpose. What's at the core?

Long before the issue of entrepreneurs choosing the wrong market haunted me, the issue of not knowing what to sell or how to sell it was what kept me up at night. After stumbling through the long and involved process of figuring it out myself, it pained me to see other entrepreneurs taking shots in the dark when it came to understanding what their markets wanted. They were providing products to customers whom they knew nothing about, and sometimes their ventures worked, but most of the time they didn't. (Hence, the well-established failure rate of small businesses in America.)

If you don't know anything about your core audience, how could you possibly know what products they want to buy? How could you know the right way to communicate with them? As much time, effort, and resources as we entrepreneurs spend on creating our actual products, we should be spending an equal amount of time and energy ensuring that we're creating something our core audiences are actually looking for. It comes down to the easiest of fixes: find out what people want and give it to them. It's that simple. But like most things in life, the devil is in the details. The nuances matter. And there's a *process*.

The foolproof way to go about this is what my book *Ask* (and corresponding ASK Method Masterclass, which goes even *deeper*) is all about. And I'm about to give you the free CliffsNotes version. Instead of the in-depth and tactical format the book and course offer, I'm going to give you a high-level breakdown of the ASK Method, because I want you to feel like you have a full tool chest as you move from your business idea to your business launch.

After you've chosen your market, ASK is a somewhat counterintuitive marketing methodology to first, figure out exactly what your customers want to buy; second, successfully launch your business out of the gate with minimum risk; and third, create a mass of raving fans in the process.

The ASK Method starts with the desire to better understand your market at a deep emotional level so you can ultimately better sell and better serve your market. Knowing your market at this deep emotional level requires asking the *right* questions in the *right* way to understand what your most ideal potential customers want. Not what they *think* they want, not what they *say* they want, but what they *really* want. And most importantly, what they really want to *buy*.

Henry Ford is thought to have said, "If I had asked people what they wanted, they would've told me faster horses . . ." Steve Jobs is attributed as saying, "People don't know what they want until you show it to them . . ." And the reason why these statements *ring* true is because they *are* true. People don't know what they *want*. But they *do* know one thing, and that's this: They *do* know what they *don't* want. And therein lies the first *clue* to figuring out what to ask. The *right* questions are somewhat counterintuitive.

Let me give you an example:

One of the first steps in the ASK Method after you've chosen your market is to run what we call a Deep Dive Survey. A Deep Dive Survey, or DDS, includes a series of questions that follow a very specific format designed to uncover what to sell or create in your newly chosen market. One of those questions is what we call the SMIQ, which stands for *Single Most Important Question*, because as the name implies, this is your single most important question (creative name, I know). At this point in your entrepreneurial journey, as you'll see in a moment, you're already halfway through creating your SMIQ.

Now, the SMIQ itself *also* follows a very specific format. In fact, when I introduce it to you, you may recognize this question, because, quite literally, thousands of companies around the world now use the ASK Method as an integral part of their business. So there's every chance one of them has already asked you this question. It goes like this: "When it comes to *X*, what's your single biggest challenge, frustration, or question you've been struggling with? (Please be as detailed and specific as possible.)"

Now here's the cool part:

See that *X*?

That *X* gets replaced with . . .

Your Bullseye Keyword!

Yep, the same one you've been working so hard to arrive at here in this book.

(I told you it was important!)

So here's how the process works:

First, you take your Bullseye Keyword based on the market you've chosen, whether that Bullseye Keyword is "learn Chinese," "improve memory," "orchid care," or whatever it may be.

Let's say for the purpose of this example, your Bullseye Keyword is "potty train puppy."

You then insert your Bullseye Keyword into the SMIQ format:

"When it comes to potty training your puppy, what's your single biggest challenge, frustration, or question you've been struggling with? (Please be as detailed and specific as possible.)"

Of course, you may need to tweak the format of your keyword slightly, so it grammatically works and makes sense in this sentence form.

Now, the reason for asking this question in this *specific* way, is because, as we now know, while people don't know what they want, they *do* know what they *don't* want. People might not be able to tell you everything they're looking for in their dream car. But they can and *will* very accurately tell you what the most frustrating, annoying thing is about the car they're driving right now. Or in this case, the thing they're most frustrated about when it comes to potty training their puppy. In other words, they'll tell you exactly what they want, if you just know how to ask.

When you ask people this question, whether through a survey link created in a survey software like bucket.io designed for this very process, or through a simple Facebook post, you want the response format of this question to be open-ended—that is, they can write their response in their own words, as opposed to selecting one of several multiple choice options. The reason for keeping this question open-ended is that it's all about discovering who the "hyper-responsive" potential customers are in your market—the people most motivated and interested and likely to *spend money* to solve the problem that you're intending to solve. It's about uncovering what natural language patterns these hyper-responsives use, so you can echo that language back in your marketing and messaging. It's about identifying what makes the hyper-responsive people in your market different from everyone else so you can focus 100 percent of your effort on targeting and serving similar customers.

One of the ways in which you can identify hyper-responsives is, in part, by looking at the length of their response to your SMIQ. All things being equal, the person who gives a longer, more detailed, more passionate response to the question "What's your single biggest frustration?" is more likely to spend money on a product that *solves* that frustration than the person who gives you a short one- or two-word answer.

This is where the ASK Method begins, but it doesn't end there.

From here, you can begin identifying the common themes you hear over and over again among your hyper-responsives. This helps you identify the different segments of your market, or "buckets" as we call them (most markets have three to five), and what makes each bucket different. You can then figure out what buckets to focus on, decide which ones you should ignore, and discover the unique needs, wants, and desires of the people in each of those individual buckets.

See how everything starts to come together?

And do you see how by asking these questions up front, just like with the Choose Method, you're mitigating your risk and setting yourself up to succeed right out of the gate by stacking the deck in your favor?

By doing this work up front, when it comes time to launch your website, you will have set yourself up to be able to communicate with each bucket *differently*—by *asking* people to answer a few simple questions when they first arrive on your website in an automated way. This allows you to customize your communication, not only on your website, but also in your e-mails and social media.

This does not necessarily mean you need to come up with different products for each of your buckets. In fact, this is where can you tap into another aspect of the ASK Method, the power of *perceived customization,* where you might sell one single product or service but talk about that product on your website *in different ways* based on which bucket someone lands in. You could create a specific webpage for each bucket, each one covering slightly different features and benefits of your product, sharing different case studies and success stories, all based on the unique needs, wants, and desires of that specific bucket.

So instead of trying to guess who someone is when they land on your website, and communicate with everyone in the same "one-size-fits-all" fashion, you first take the time to *ask* a few simple questions. Then based on the answers to those questions, you can direct people to a different page on your website based on their response, enabling you to speak their *exact* language and offer them the exact product or service they want and need.

Does that seem like a bit of work?

Well, frankly, it is. But, just like the Choose Method, the ASK Method is a similarly structured, step-by-step process. And while rigorous, just like *Choose,* it's designed to mitigate your risk so you don't waste time and money building something that nobody wants to buy. Before you build, you *ask*.

Like *Choose, Ask* offers a method that also represents simplicity on the far side of complexity, and one that demystifies, arguably, the single biggest question every entrepreneur faces after they *choose their market* and that's this:

How do I figure out exactly what people want to buy and give it to them so I can be successful right from the start?

The ASK Method sets you up for that success. Because instead of guessing what people want, you *know* what they want. Instead of communicating in a "one-size-fits-all" way, you begin by putting people into buckets, so you can customize your messaging based on their situation. Instead of sounding like an outsider, you speak the insider language of your hyper-responsives. You know what your customers' biggest pains and frustrations are, as well as their deepest wants, needs, and desires.

You've gone to such great lengths because your desire is not only to better sell, but to better serve. And the result? Your drive to understand your market leaves your customers feeling understood. And when people feel understood, that's when they fall in love with you and your business; that's when they become massive, raving fans for life; and that's when they look to buy from you . . . again and again and again. Because as the saying goes, people don't care how much you know until they know how much you care. And *that* is how you add a warm personal touch in a cold digital world.

So what's your next step? Where do you go from here? Well, once you *Choose,* your next step . . . is to *Ask.*

Progress Summary

You've just completed Stage 3 in the Choose Method Process!

Here's a quick summary of your progress.

Stage 1—BRAINSTORM

☑ Step 1—Model Brainstorm

☑ Step 2—Market Brainstorm

☑ Step 3—Business Idea Brainstorm

STAGE 2—TEST

☑ Step 4—Bullseye Keyword

☑ Step 5—Market Size Sweet Spot

☑ Step 6—Market Competition Sweet Spot

☑ Step 7—Market Must-Haves

STAGE 3—CHOOSE

☑ Step 8—Choose Your Market

☑ Step 9—The Final Step to Launch—The ASK Method

Epilogue

Before we end, there is one final piece of advice
I'd like to leave you with, and that's this:
It's something I originally wrote for my two boys,
Henry and Bradley.
But I wanted to share it with you here.
Because it's too important not to.
In fact, if you take nothing else from what I've shared,
these might be the important words you read
in this entire book.
So here goes . . .

▲ ▲ ▲

When you're older.
Not now, but someday, perhaps.
If you decide to become an entrepreneur
just like your mom and dad . . .
I want to share with you,
what I wish I knew when I was a young man.

▲ ▲ ▲

The times you'll be most fulfilled,
the times when you'll be happiest,
are not the times when you hit some lofty
goal or milestone.
For a moment, maybe yes.
But those moments are fleeting.
Moments when you make your first sale.

Make your first million dollars.
Or have your first million-dollar day.
Those moments will come and go.
And if you're not careful . . .
you'll find yourself in a never-ending chase,
reaching after the next big milestone.
And the next one after that.
Being an entrepreneur is not about milestones.

▲　▲　▲

Being an entrepreneur is also not about
measuring up.
It's not about measuring up to anyone
else's outside standard,
whether that's from me or your mom or anyone else.
Or some unrealistically high standard you may
have set for yourself.
Don't ever compare yourself to anyone else.
This is your race to run.
And you've *got* this.
Remember that.
Always.

▲　▲　▲

Being an entrepreneur is not about Mastery.
Be careful with Mastery.
Mastery is elusive.
Mastery is a never-ending quest.
You'll spend your entire life pursuing Mastery,
and if you're not careful, one day you'll wake up
old and gray and alone.
Life is too short and precious.
Don't spend it chasing something you can't catch.

Because it can mean missing out on the
much more important stuff.
Sure, *leave it all on the field*.
But more importantly, *live and love fully*.

▲　▲　▲

Being an entrepreneur is all about one thing:
In a word, it's about *Momentum*.
Momentum means moving forward.
No matter how fast or how slow.
Momentum means progress, not perfection.
No matter how afraid you might be.
Momentum means doing as well as you
can in your business,
so you can do as much good as you can in the world.
So you can give back.
So you can make an impact.
And not waiting for someday to get started with that.
But starting right here, right now, today.

▲　▲　▲

Being an entrepreneur is not about arriving at
some magical destination.
Or finally "making it" one day.
It's about enjoying the whole entire messy
journey itself.
It's about enjoying the ride.
It's about tossing your boat in the river.
And savoring the wind in your face and the
wild white water.
It's embracing the struggle.
It's about enjoying the flow.

It's about soaking it all in while you're in the middle of it all.
Because in life, you've only got one shot.
So whatever you're going to do, now is the time to do it.
Don't let fear slow you down.
The only regret I have in life is when I let fear hold me back.
Constantly remind yourself:
There is no such thing as failure.
You only win or you learn.
Although winning is a little more fun. :-)

▲ ▲ ▲

And when you do toss your boat in that river . . .
and the water gets rough.
When you're low on courage.
And even lower on grit.
When you're feeling . . .
Desperate.
Defeated.
Done.
And when I'm not there to save you.
If your boat flips.
If it capsizes.
If you're tossed in cold, frigid water, and you're all alone.
If you feel like you're drowning.
If you feel like you've lost your way.
If you feel completely overwhelmed.
Remember these three words:
Just.
Keep.
Swimming.

▲ ▲ ▲

So.
If you *do* decide to become an entrepreneur . . .
(And even if you *don't* . . .)
The secret to being happy?
The secret to being fulfilled?
Is to constantly seek momentum.
Seek progress, not perfection.
Enjoy the journey.
Enjoy the ride.
And no matter what happens.
Just. Keep. Swimming.
Because whenever you're reading this,
wherever you're reading this,
I'll tell you right here, right now,
you've *got* this.
Seriously, you do.
And no matter what, remember:
I love you with all my heart, and I always will.

Love,
Dad

▲ ▲ ▲

Bonus Resources

Download Your Bonus Resources

Each of the following resources are available for free in your Bonus Online Resource Area, which you can find at: www.choosethebook.com/bonuses.

In sharing them here, I want to provide you with a clear description of each resource to make it easier for you to find what you need, so the website can provide you with a one-stop shop for all your Choose Your Market needs, now and in the future.

25 Profitable Niche Ideas

This list gives you 25 ideas for lucrative market niches that fit within the Market Sweet Spot. For years I kept this top-secret list tightly guarded because it represented the markets I planned on going into. Now, even though I am exclusively focused on teaching and serving entrepreneurs, this list is still incredibly valuable, and I have extracted 25 of the most profitable business ideas for you as thought-starters and inspiration.

Model Brainstorm Worksheet

This resource will guide you as you brainstorm the various *education and expertise* business models available to you, including Product Focused, Client Focused, Membership Focused, Event Focused.

One-Page Business Model Worksheet

This resource provides a one-page visual overview of the IN/UP/MAX business model, whereby you offer an entry-level product that 100 percent of your customers buy, then a mid-level product priced 10 times higher that approximately 10 percent of your customers buy, and finally a high-end or premium product priced 100 times higher than the entry-level product that approximately 1 percent of your customers buy.

Market Brainstorm Worksheet

This resource is a starting place for you to think about the market you might want to focus on. It is a *brainstorm* process worksheet, which means there are no "bad" ideas. Just get all your thoughts down for each of the "brainstorm prompts," including the Four Entrepreneur Types: Mission Based, Passion Based, Opportunity Based, and Undecided.

Business Idea Brainstorm Worksheet

This resource provides your business idea brainstorm with structure for recording your best ideas, making sure they fit into the "I want to help people _____" framework and prioritizing them based on your Entrepreneur Type.

Choosing Your Green Light Market Worksheet

This three-checkpoint resource will guide you through the entire Test Stage of the Choose Method, including your Market Size Sweet Spot test, Market Competition Sweet Spot test, and Five Market Must-Haves test. It sets you up perfectly for the final Stage, where you get to Choose the right market.

Assessment

What Type of Business Should You Start?

Use the What Type of Business Should You Start? Assessment to gain clarity around which type of business is most suited to your Entrepreneur Type and which product is the best fit for you based on your personality, your strengths, preferences, and objectives.

Full-Color Screenshots of All Graphs and Pages

Get full-color screenshots of all the graphs and pages referenced throughout the book. In particular, the Google Trends data really comes to life, and the distinctions are even more powerful, when you can see it in color.

(🐧) You can get all these resources right now over in your Bonus Online Resource Area at www.choosethebook .com/bonuses.

Glossary

Addition by subtraction — the idea that by eliminating possibilities and distractions and focusing on doing fewer things in a better, deeper, and more focused way, you can actually accomplish more, faster.

AFOL — adult fan of LEGO. The most common term used to refer to LEGO fans who are adults. :-)

Amazon "Sponsored Listings" — paid product listings on Amazon.com. The number of sponsored listings selling education and expertise on the first page of results helps determine whether your Bullseye Keyword falls in the Competition Sweet Spot.

Analysis Paralysis — the state when overthinking a situation results in lack of action.

ASK Method® — the marketing methodology designed to figure out exactly what your customers want to buy, successfully launch your business, and, in the process, create a mass of raving fans—all designed to help you better sell to your market and better serve that market.

Ask Method, Deep Dive Survey (DDS) — a series of questions that follows a very specific format designed to uncover what your market wants and how to sell it to them; to understand your market at a deep emotional level, revealing the natural consumer language used to describe their needs, wants, and desires; to separate the hyper-responsive segment of that market from everyone else; and to identify the most important buckets of hyper-responsives to focus on in that market.

Ask Method, Hyper-Responsives — the people most motivated, interested, and likely to spend money to solve the problem that you're intending to solve and that you are asking about in your Deep Dive Survey. They're determined, in part, by measuring the depth of their answers to your SMIQ.

Ask Method, Perceived Customization — the process by which you sell a single product or service but talk about it in different ways, highlighting distinct features, benefits, and customer success stories so each customer experiences it as being "just for them."

Ask Method, Single Most Important Question (SMIQ) — the single most important question in your Deep Dive Survey that is open-ended and designed to identify your hyper-responsives, your most important buckets, and the language to use in your marketing and messaging.

Audience — your customers, readers, subscribers, and followers within your chosen market or niche.

Brainstorming — the process of generating and gathering ideas without judgment, and then filtering them to find the best options.

Bucket.io® — the leading, easy-to-use marketing funnel software for building surveys, quizzes, and funnels designed to segment people into buckets so you can both discover what your most important buckets are as well as customize your messaging to each of those buckets.

Buckets — the primary segments or groups of people in your chosen market or niche. By putting people into different buckets, you can speak to their unique needs, wants, and desires based on what sets of challenges they face, which situations they come across, or what stage they are at in their journey.

Business Model — the way in which you go about generating revenue and profit in your business.

Choose Method™ — the marketing methodology outlined in this book that will help you figure out what market to go into and what business to start. It is designed to give you clarity and confidence, so you can take the leap and get started.

Continuity Income — income you generate by making a single sale that pays you over and over again, such as charging a monthly, recurring subscription.

E-learning — short for "electronic learning." This includes educational courses, workshops, and programs that are delivered online.

Education and Expertise — a business model whereby you package ideas, information, and/or expertise (or the expertise of others) into products and services, such as digital courses and books, coaching and consulting, membership sites, and live events. It is a highly recommended business model for many people who want to start their own business or be their own boss, because of its low overhead, low barriers to start-up, and high profit margins.

Entrepreneur Type — a framework designed to help figure out what type of business to start based on your natural tendencies.

Entrepreneur Type, Mission Based — an entrepreneur who has a clear and specific mission they feel called to pursue.

Entrepreneur Type, Opportunity Based — an entrepreneur who finds and follows a new area of opportunity and growth.

Entrepreneur Type, Passion Based — an entrepreneur who is fueled by a passion that revolves around a topic or subject matter they love.

Entrepreneur Type, Undecided — an entrepreneur who isn't sure about what type of business to start.

Evergreen Revenue — income you generate by building a system that produces consistent, ongoing sales of a product or service on a daily or weekly basis, without much additional work after the initial, upfront investment and outlay of effort. This can serve as a foundation of your business.

Extrovert — a generally outgoing, overtly expressive person who derives energy from being around and interacting with other people.

Google Trends — a free tool that shows how often a particular search term is entered into Google relative to the total worldwide search volume. It gives a benchmark of the popularity and relevance of your Bullseye Keyword.

"I Want to" Statement — a simple statement designed to help you clearly articulate how you will serve people within the business you're considering starting.

IN/UP/MAX — a progressive framework that helps you design three ascending levels of products or services for your chosen business model.

Introvert — a generally shy and reticent person, especially around large groups of people, who recharges and derives energy from being alone.

Keyword Phrase — a short phrase describing what you do or what is at the core of what you offer. Within the context of the Choose Method, in the Test Stage, Keyword Phrases are added to your "I want to help people . . ." statement to articulate the process, transformation, or result you want to deliver to your market.

Keyword, Bullseye — a one- to three-word version of your Keyword Phrase that expresses the process, journey, or transformation people will experience as a result of buying your product.

Keywords, Rosetta Stone — a unique combination of four specific Bullseye Keywords that, when entered into Google Trends, determines the Market Size Sweet Spot.

Market — the group of people you choose to serve in your business—your "who."

Market Must-Haves — the five required attributes of a market that are generally necessary for a business idea to be successful and sustainable for the long-term.

Market Must-Haves, $10,000 Problem — an urgent problem that has a high pain point attached to it and that can, under certain circumstances, become a huge problem that causes people to want to solve it immediately, with little price sensitivity toward purchasing a solution.

Market Must-Haves, Future Problem — additional future problems you can solve in the same market, for the same customer, above and beyond that first problem you might solve for them.

Market Must-Haves, Players With Money (PWMs) — people willing to spend a large sum of money in one area of their lives to address or avoid a recurring problem, or to fuel an important goal, hobby, or personal vision.

Market, Enthusiast — a market where the buyers are interested in the subject in such a way that they tend to remain buyers of products and services for a long period of time. Examples include dog ownership and weight loss.

Market, Evergreen — a market with decades-long longevity and one that is continually relevant, not threatened by external forces like cultural shifts, a temperamental economy, or fleeting interest. Examples include gardening and business growth.

Market, Fad — a market that has a brief introductory period when the product suddenly hits the market, a growth stage when the product sky-rockets into market acceptance, and then a sharp downward decline. Examples include "fidget spinners" and "bitcoin."

Market, Greenlight — a market that passes all the tests in the Choose Method and that is safe to explore pursuing further as a potentially viable business idea.

Market, Problem / Solution — a market in which once buyers solve their problem, they move on with their lives and no longer remain interested in the subject or in purchasing additional products and services. Examples include mold removal and flood recovery.

Momentum — moving forward consistently, no matter how fast or slow.

Niche — a niche typically represents a subset of people within a larger market. For example, "open water scuba divers" represents a subset of the "scuba divers" market and "homeschooling parents" represents a subset of the "parents" market.

Practice Business — a business in which you are not personally attached to the subject matter or results but which you start with the intent of focusing on learning the "process" of building a business. If you are stuck on deciding what business to start, beginning with a Practice Business can help lessen the stress and pressure you might feel to make the "right" choice of market or business.

Product — something a business sells. In the context of selling education and expertise, a product can represent anything from a physical product, such as a book; a digital program, such as an online course; or even a service, such as a coaching program.

Product Grid — the grid outlining the four quadrants you can focus on when selling education and expertise. The quadrants include Product, Client, Membership, and Event Focused.

Product Grid, Client Focused Quadrant — the quadrant that focuses on working with a small number of clients in a deep and focused way. Examples include private consulting, hosting a mastermind group, or running a group coaching program.

Product Grid, Event Focused Quadrant — the quadrant that focuses on any concentrated event, either online or in person, where people are getting together in one place and that begins and ends within a succinct period of time.

Product Grid, Membership Focused Quadrant — the quadrant that focuses on building a community of people, typically online. Examples include membership sites and online networking groups that are designed to generate Continuity Income.

Product Grid, Product Focused Quadrant — the quadrant that focuses on productizing your expertise. The "product" can be physical, like a book, but is most often digital, like an e-book or online course.

Profit Margin — the amount by which revenue from sales exceeds costs in a business.

Sweet Spot, Market Competition — a market that has the right number of competitors—not too many, but not too few. The Market Competition Sweet Spot is determined by measuring the amount of advertising in your market through Amazon.com.

Sweet Spot, Market Size — a specific, narrow range in search volume on a Google Trends graph representing the ideal market size, which is determined by comparing your Bullseye Keyword with several Rosetta Stone Keywords.

Test, Amazon — a "first pass" check to confirm that your Bullseye Keyword matches what people are actually looking to purchase on Amazon.

Test, Google — a "first pass" check to confirm that your Bullseye Keyword matches what people are actually searching for on Google.

Tests, First Pass — the Google and Amazon tests that give you a quick indication whether your Bullseye Keyword is potentially viable.

Tests, Sweet Spot — the Market Size and Market Competition tests that help determine if your market has a unique combination of being the right size and having the right amount of competition.

Notes

START HERE

1. U.S. Department of Labor, Bureau of Labor Statistics, "Business Employment Dynamics," April 28, 2016. https://www.bls.gov/bdm/entrepreneurship/entrepreneurship.htm.

STAGE 1

1. Alex F. Osborn, *How to "Think Up"* (New York, London: McGraw-Hill Book Co., 1942).

STAGE 1: STEP 1

1. https://elearningindustry.com/new-report-on-e-learning-market-trends-and-forecast-2014-2016-just-released

2. https://www.reuters.com/brandfeatures/venture-capital/article?id=11353

3. Wikipedia, "International Chamber of Commerce," December 17, 2018. https://en.wikipedia.org/wiki/International_Chamber_of_Commerce.

STAGE 2: STEP 4

1. Google and the Google logo are registered trademarks of Google LLC, used with permission.

2. Google and the Google logo are registered trademarks of Google LLC, used with permission.

STAGE 2: STEP 5

1. Because the Google Trends platform may be subject to change, for the latest updates to factor these changes into your calculations for this test, be sure to visit the Bonus Online Resource Area for any critical updates to the Market Size Sweet Spot Test.

2. Google and the Google logo are registered trademarks of Google LLC, used with permission.

3. "Everything you ever wanted to know about the Rosetta Stone," *British Museum Blog*, 2017. https://blog .britishmuseum.org/everything-you-ever-wanted-to-know -about-the-rosetta-stone.

STAGE 2: STEP 6

1. Ingrid Lunden, "Amazon's share of the US e-commerce market is now 49%, or 5% of all retail spend," TechCrunch, July 2018. https://techcrunch.com/2018/ 07/13/amazons-share-of-the-us-e-commerce-market-is -now-49-or-5-of-all-retail-spend.

2. Because Amazon is always changing its platform, for the latest updates to factor these changes into your calculations for this test, be sure to visit the Bonus Online Resource Area for any critical updates to the Market Competition Sweet Spot Test.

STAGE 2: STEP 7

1. Press release, "iPhone 4S First Weekend Sales Top Four Million," Apple Newsroom, October 17, 2011. https:// www.apple.com/newsroom/2011/10/17iPhone-4S-First -Weekend-Sales-Top-Four-Million.

2. Masashi Soga, Kevin J. Gaston, and Yuichi Yamaura, "Gardening is beneficial for health: A meta-analysis." *Preventive Medicine Reports* 5, March 2017, 92–99. https://www.ncbi.nlm.nih.gov/pmc/articles/ PMC5153451/#bb0265.

3. Erik Matuszewski, "Golf Channel Acquires Revolution Golf, Boosting Digital Audience To 15 Million," *Forbes,* August 7, 2017. https://www.forbes.com/sites/erikmatuszewski/2017/08/07/golf-channel-acquires-revolution-golf-boosting-digital-audience-to-15-million.

4. Chateau Poochie website. http://www.chateaupoochie.com/index.htm.

5. Canis Resort website. https://www.canisresort.com/en/the-resort.

6. Annabel Fenwick Elliot, "We're in for a ruff flight! Japanese airline now allows passengers to travel with their dogs in the main cabin," *Daily Mail,* January 27, 2017. https://www.dailymail.co.uk/travel/travel_news/article-4164644/Japan-Airlines-allows-dogs-passenger-cabin.html.

Acknowledgments

In my first book, *Ask*, I mentioned they say it takes a village to raise a child, and that writing a book like this takes not just a village, but an entire metropolis. I believe that to be truer today than ever. In fact, it's almost unfair to list only one name on the cover of a book like this because of the amount of work, support, and contribution that has come from so many people, without whom this book would not have been possible. And while it would be impossible to thank *everyone* who had an impact on this book, there are a few people who deserve specific mention here.

First, my wife, Tylene, for supporting me and being by my side since day one. We have been together over half our lives, and none of what you've read about in this book would've been remotely possible without her incredible sacrifice and support. From building a company that now impacts millions of lives to building an incredible life and family together, I will forever look back so grateful you let me walk you home after class that day on campus nearly 20 years ago.

To my two boys, Henry and Bradley. If this book is all about choosing your who, you are unequivocally my *why*. Getting to be your dad is the greatest gift I've ever been given.

My parents, Paul and Joanne, and my sister, Allison, thank you for always being there for me. My parents deserve all the credit for everything you've read about in this book. We all stand on the shoulders of giants, and the sacrifices they made, the example they set, and the work ethic and values they taught me at a young age are what led to making this book and all the impact it has in this world a reality.

To my extended family, including my brother-in-law, Pat, for taking great care of my only sister. My wife's family, especially my sister-in-law, Clara, and mother-in-law, Maria, for taking great care of our boys on so many occasions, and my entire extended family: Thank you. I love you all.

Next on the list is Michelle Falzon. If there is one person who put more time into this book than I did myself, it is Michelle. The all-nighters, the hundred-hour work weeks, the care, love, and attention you put into every single page, paragraph, and word in this book. I couldn't have done it without you, Michelle. It is rare to find someone who is your perfect creative complement, and I am just so grateful for the opportunity to work with you in this life. I've said it before and I'll say it again. You are incredible. Thank you. For everything.

My business partner, Richard Cussons. On that fateful day, when I told you I need a Richard, you were right; there is only *one* of you. I'm so grateful life connected us, I only wish it were sooner. From the bottom of my heart, I love you like a brother. And I'm so grateful to be on this journey with you. While it may be my name on the cover of this book, you deserve all the credit for the company we've built together. And this is just the beginning.

There are so many teachers, mentors who shaped my thinking, whose work influenced what you've read about in these pages, but there is one man I want to thank here, and that is my single most important mentor, Dr. Glenn Livingston. The impact Dr. Glenn has had on my life, on my thinking, and on my work is immeasurable. Millions of men and women in this world have transformed their lives because of your work, Dr. Glenn. Mine being just one. Thank you.

Thank you to Brent Cole and Krista Morgan for all your amazing work on this manuscript—you were able to take the messy thoughts and ideas swimming around in my head and transform them into something I could never have done on my own—and to Tim Pedersen for bringing the graphics, worksheets, and images to life in a way beyond my imagination.

To Alexis Fedor, Anna Baumgartner, Dr. Beverly Yates, Chad Collins, Charlie Wallace, Dana Obleman and Mike Matthewson, Jamal and Natasha Miller, Kristi Kennedy, Lex Case, Michael Hyatt, Robert Torres, Ron Reich, Sean Bissell, and Stu McLaren, thank you for openly sharing your stories and allowing me to include them to inspire others to follow in your footsteps.

To my agents, Scott Hoffman and Steve Troha, I'm so grateful for your belief in me, your belief in this book, and your patience and guidance every step of the way. Simply put, this book would not have happened were it not for you. Thank you.

To Reid Tracy at Hay House, Inc., as well as Margarete Nielsen, I could not have dreamed of better partners to work with and to help introduce this book into the world. I am so incredibly grateful for both our friendship and our partnership. And to the entire team at Hay House, especially my editor, Lisa Cheng, not only for your flexibility and patience with me but also for holding this project to your incredibly high editorial standards. And also, Patty Gift, Lindsay McGinty, Diane Thomas, Nick Welch, Marlene Robinson, Steve Morris, and the entire Hay House team, as well as Joshua Aaron for your help with the audiobook.

Special thanks to my incredible team: Everyone part of the #TeamASK family both past and present, especially Elliott, Chris, Ian, Kyle, Danielle, Tracy, Mary, Robert, Heba, Melissa, Gary, Carlos, Enrique, Tom, Antonio, Terry, Erika, Ali, Kimberly, Megan S., Kelli, Christina, Vera, Brian, Christa, Pam, Joellee, Lain, Jo, Megan O., Tim, Alex, Emmi, and all our coaches including, Natty, Nikolai, Peter, Iczel, Martha, Duncan, John, Alison, and Sean as well as Doug, Claudia, Dan, Janet, Jacqueline, and Rebecca, and everyone part of the #TeamBUCKET family. You guys set the bar both in terms of excellence and how much you care for our customers. I've never had the opportunity to work with a more amazing group of men and women in my life.

To all my friends, partners, and colleagues who read and provided early feedback on the manuscript, including Anik Singal, Annie Pratt, Brendon Burchard, Brian Kurtz, Chris Ducker, Dean Graziosi, Dorie Clark, Eben Pagan, Garrett Gunderson, Hal Elrod, James Schramko, Jason Friedman, Jay Abraham, Jeff Walker, John Assaraf, John Warrilow, Josh Turner, Kevin Harrington, Mark Ford, Mark Timm, Michael Hyatt, Mike Michalowicz, Nicholas Kusmich, Pat Flynn, Perry Marshall, Ray Edwards, Roger Dooley, Ryan Deiss, Sally Hogshead, Selena Soo, Todd Herman, Tom Ziglar, and Victoria Labalme, thank you so much for your feedback and support and for making this a better book than it would've been without you.

And to all my friends, students, and partners not already mentioned who are committed to supporting the launch of this book in a huge way, I am so grateful for you sharing the message in this book to your community, to your audience, and through your platform. You are a big part of this book, and I am so thankful for your incredible support.

To all my coaching clients, working with you, seeing you grow, overcome struggle, and push yourself as entrepreneurs to achieve freedom, make an impact, and leave your legacy is what gets me out of bed each day—and the opportunity to celebrate your success is the reason why I do what I do. Pure and simple. Thank you for allowing me to play a small role in your journey.

And lastly, to all my students and readers and everyone part of the Choose and Ask family, when I walked out of the hospital and was given a second chance after nearly slipping into a coma and dying at 30 years old, I asked myself, *What do I want to do with the rest of my life?* The answer came down to one word: Teach. Thank you for giving me the opportunity to spend my life doing what I love.

I'll leave you with the same words I share often with my two boys:

Be curious. Ask questions. Seek Truth.

Now, go out there and change the world.

About the Author

Ryan Levesque is the *Inc.* 500 CEO of The ASK Method® Company, an entrepreneur, and the #1 national best-selling author of *Ask*, which was named by *Inc.* as the #1 Marketing Book of the Year and by *Entrepreneur* as the #2 Must-Read Book for Budding Entrepreneurs. His work has been featured in *The Wall Street Journal*, *USA Today*, *Forbes*, and *Entrepreneur*, and over 250,000 entrepreneurs subscribe to his email newsletter offering business advice. He is also a co-founder and investor in bucket.io®, a leading marketing funnel software for entrepreneurs.

A certified AFOL (Adult Fan of LEGO), Ryan lives with his wife, Tylene, and their two boys in Austin, Texas. You can follow his work at www.askmethod.com.

Hay House Titles of Related Interest

THE SHIFT, the movie,
starring Dr. Wayne W. Dyer
(available as a 1-DVD program, an expanded 2-DVD set,
and an online streaming video)
Learn more at www.hayhouse.com/the-shift-movie

▲ ▲ ▲

BRING YOUR WHOLE SELF TO WORK, by Mike Robbins

*HIGH PERFORMANCE HABITS: How Extraordinary People
Become That Way,* by Brendon Burchard

PURPOSE: Find Your Truth and Embrace Your Calling,
by Jessica Huie

*THE SACRED SIX: The Simple, Step-by-Step Process for Focusing
Your Attention & Recovering Your Dreams,* by J. B. Glossinger,
M.B.A., Ph.D.

All of the above are available at your local bookstore,
or may be ordered by contacting Hay House (see next page).

▲ ▲ ▲

We hope you enjoyed this Hay House book. If you'd like to receive our online catalog featuring additional information on Hay House books and products, or if you'd like to find out more about the Hay Foundation, please contact:

Hay House, Inc., P.O. Box 5100, Carlsbad, CA 92018-5100
(760) 431-7695 or (800) 654-5126
(760) 431-6948 (fax) or (800) 650-5115 (fax)
www.hayhouse.com® • www.hayfoundation.org

———

Published in Australia by:
Hay House Australia Pty. Ltd., 18/36 Ralph St., Alexandria NSW 2015
Phone: 612-9669-4299 • *Fax:* 612-9669-4144 • www.hayhouse.com.au

Published in the United Kingdom by:
Hay House UK, Ltd., Astley House, 33 Notting Hill Gate, London W11 3JQ
Phone: 44-20-3675-2450 • *Fax:* 44-20-3675-2451 • www.hayhouse.co.uk

Published in India by: Hay House Publishers India,
Muskaan Complex, Plot No. 3, B-2, Vasant Kunj, New Delhi 110 070
Phone: 91-11-4176-1620 • *Fax:* 91-11-4176-1630 • www.hayhouse.co.in

———

Access New Knowledge.
Anytime. Anywhere.

Learn and evolve at your own pace
with the world's leading experts.

www.hayhouseU.com